Off Script

Off Script

Living Out Loud

Marci Ien

Collins

Published by Collins, an imprint of HarperCollins Publishers Ltd

First edition

HarperCollins books may be purchased for educational, business
or sales promotional use through our Special Markets Department.

HarperCollins Publishers Ltd
Bay Adelaide Centre, East Tower
22 Adelaide Street West, 41st Floor
Toronto, Ontario, Canada
M5H 4E3

www.harpercollins.ca

All photos courtesy of the author except the following, which are
© Caitlin Connelly/*The Social*: pages 141, 186 and 211.

Library and Archives Canada Cataloguing in Publication
Title: Off script : living out loud / Marci Ien.
Names: Ien, Marci, author.
Identifiers: Canadiana (print) 20200285246 | Canadiana (ebook)
20200285289 | ISBN 9781443460088
(hardcover) | ISBN 9781443460095 (ebook)
Subjects: LCSH: Self-realization. | LCSH: Self-actualization (Psychology) |
LCSH: Satisfaction. |
LCSH: Happiness. | LCSH: Conduct of life.
Classification: LCC BF637.S4 I36 2020 | DDC 158.1—dc23

Printed and bound in the United States of America
LSC/H 9 8 7 6 5 4 3 2 1

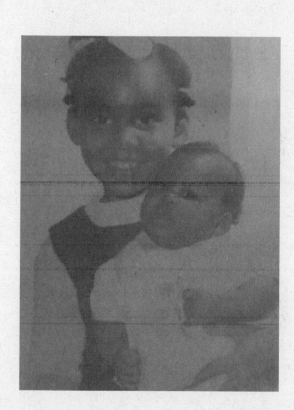

To Lowi. It's always been us.

I believe that the most important legacy is how we live on in other people. Were we kind? Did we open another's mind to a different way of seeing? Did we love and were we loved?

—Teva Harrison

Off Script

Lessons from my father

My dad walked onto the stage in the high-school gymnasium carrying a cut-out of a tombstone.

A giant of a man in a grey suit, he looked out at the rows and rows of students assembled: *his* students, the young men and women at the school where he was principal, the adolescents he hoped to inspire and lead toward opportunity and success. My dad stood on that stage in his grey suit, looking for all the world like Morgan Freeman in the movie *Lean on Me*—I swear, looking back, I can almost hear Axl Rose belting out "Welcome to the Jungle." Because that's how I still see him, my dad: staring down any rough elements, wanting to be everything he could be to those kids.

He was up there, larger than life, showing no sign of the strain of running a large school. His face bore no hint of his worries for his students' prospects. He looked at those hundreds of young people with their whole lives stretched out before them, and he waved that tombstone, and he shouted out, in a voice that filled the gym: "What's the most important part of this?"

I was in middle school, maybe twelve years old, hanging around at his high school for the day, as I often did when there was a PA day at my own school in Scarborough, Ontario. It wasn't unusual for me, on such a day, to find myself in a gym full of high schoolers. My dad was one of those principals who liked holding assemblies: he really liked bringing his kids together. I looked around me. Those students, all older than I was, thought the answer was easy.

They shouted back: "The day you were born!"

They screamed out: "The day you die!"

They yelled: "Your name!"

My dad was like that: he could really grab a room. Even this gymnasium full of what might have been restless, unruly students. Now that he had them, he told them what he most wanted them to hear: No, he told them. (Told us, I should say. I was caught, too, just like the kids around me, hanging on his every word.)

It's not what you think, he said.

The most important part is the smallest part. The dash. The time you spend on this earth. All the years that come between the two dates are compressed in that dash. And that has to count. It has to mean something. You have to leave some mark in life.

What we have to consider is that we're here for a purpose. We have to find that purpose, and not let people or events deter us. We have to push forward and progress. And that's all part of the dash.

That day was nearly forty years ago, but Dad's message, seeing him up there and the pride I felt, has never left me. I even named my son Dash. He fits the bill. He's a bright light. He moves quickly and fearlessly. (My daughter, Blaize, lives up to *her* fiery name, too. I named her after the word "trailblazer.") My dad is like me: he doesn't use notes when he speaks. He gets his thoughts together, looks for inspiration. Then he freestyles. Back then, he'd come across Linda Ellis's poem "The Dash," which has become famous because of its message about the true value of a life. He incorporated that idea into his speech. But here's the beauty of Dad's thinking. "The Dash" was written as a funeral poem—it was about looking back. He read that poem with its powerful message, thought it over, and switched it around. He made it not about the end of life but the beginning.

What are you going to do with your life? What kind of mark will you leave?

When Dad spoke of the "mark" we leave, he didn't just mean purpose and goals. He spoke of the people in our lives who make reaching for those goals possible. To his students he spoke especially of parents, caregivers, guardians. The people who make sacrifices every day in order to be there for you and give you what you need. *Remember that they want the best for you,* he told that gymnasium full of students, that crowd of kids that included me.

Part of using your time well, he said, *is being grateful for what you have, and even more so, who you have. Time is something you can't take for granted, absolutely. And the people you*

have with you during your time? You can't take them for granted
either. So how about saying thanks to your parents for breakfast?
Remember to say thank you to them for all that they do.

Here's what I've found: the further in life I get, the more
thank yous I need to say.

I've been thinking, lately, about what my dad said that
day. About legacy. Purpose. My time here. How I'm using my
microphone. What it means to have it. And especially about the
people in my life who've made it possible for me to be who I am
and do what I do.

In 2010, when the Olympic Winter Games came to Vancouver,
I was a news anchor for CTV's national morning show, *Canada*
AM, for which I would later serve as co-host for six years with
Beverly Thomson and Jeff Hutcheson. When it comes to the
Olympics, the whole network kicks into gear—news, sports and
entertainment divisions. I was called to duty as well: I was sent
to Halifax to take part in the Olympic torch relay.

The location was no accident. Bev had started her career in
Belleville, Ontario—that's where she was sent to carry the torch.
Co-host Seamus O'Regan (now a Liberal MP), carried the torch
in his home province, Newfoundland and Labrador. Jeff represented western Canada and carried his torch in Langley, BC.
Halifax was my city—where I'd landed my first job with the network, as a reporter for CTV News in 1997. It was there that I'd
covered major tragedies such as the crash of Swissair Flight 111
off Peggy's Cove, and stories close to my heart such as the legacy

of Africville, the Black Halifax village that was demolished in the 1960s, a blot on Canadian history.

It was amazing, absolutely amazing, to return to Halifax to be part of this Olympic ceremony. I felt a lot of pride to represent my country this way. My husband, Lloyd, and our daughter, Blaize—she was only five years old—flew east with me: this opportunity was too exciting to miss. We planned to spend a family weekend in Halifax afterward. We checked into our hotel and, as instructed, I went to meet the organizers and other participants near Citadel Hill. It was late November, cold and grey. As the relay was about to get underway, we were given our instructions and special clothing, which included a white hat and track suit and red woollen Hudson's Bay Olympic mittens. Then we all dispersed to our appointed spots on the route.

Once the torch was handed off to you, you could walk, run or jog. The key was that you were to do your part of the route solo: you're the torchbearer; it's only you.

I chose to walk. So I was right in downtown Halifax, marching down the street, torch in hand. It was long and slim, made of this hard, slippery plastic. The flame atop it burned bright. The streets were lined like a parade route. There were loads of people. Lloyd and Blaize had set up in a spot where I would pass them. All of a sudden I heard, "Momma! Momma!" I turned, and there was Blaize, bundled up in her pink scarf and furry boots. She'd spotted me, and she was shouting for all she was worth.

An RCMP officer heard Blaize calling, went over to her and with Lloyd's permission walked her over to me. I smiled at him—grateful for his kind gesture—and held her hand with my left while gripping the torch with my right. And she walked with me. I was worried; the torch was so slippery, I thought it would slip from my mittened hand. But it didn't. And we finished my leg of the relay together.

Later, one of the producers in the control room told me that, when she looked at her monitor and saw Blaize and me together, it brought tears to her eyes.

That day was emotional for me, too. I thought it was really important for me as a Black woman to be seen carrying the torch.

It made me think about the symbolic torches I've held throughout my career. You can't choose whether or not you want to be a role model. If you're in the public eye—if you have a platform—you just are one. Someone is going to be influenced by what you say or don't say. By what you do or don't do.

As a Black female news anchor—and, later, the first Black woman in Canada to co-host a morning news show—I've never felt I had a lot of room for error. I had to be great. I had to show, every day, that I deserved to be there. That I wasn't a token minority. That I had earned the opportunities I'd been given. I also wanted to be a beacon of hope, a human torch, so that kids—not just my own but any kids out there watching—can see what's possible. Who they can be. When I carried that torch and walked with my daughter in the relay, for us to be there, to be present, to be seen on national television as part of that ancient ceremony—that meant something more than just its part in the Olympics.

I think of my daughter's namesake: the word "trailblazer." I think of my dad, who left Trinidad to study at the University of

Toronto (his parents sold a parcel of land to make this possible); who won a scholarship and blazed a trail to Harvard University in Cambridge; and who then came straight back to Toronto to give to the kids here who needed it most the best of what he'd learned. More than a chance at a solid education, he gave them a role model: he gave them himself.

My dad was, and still is, a torchbearer. And he's handed that torch to me. I've accepted it, and as I did with the actual torch during the relay in Halifax, I'm holding on for dear life. I'm using it to light my way and (God willing) my children's way—and I hope I can also use it, even in a small way, to light a path for others as well.

Think of the torches we all may carry. The possibilities are immense. Even if you're not in the public eye, you can make a difference. What path will you light with your torch? What mark will you leave? What purpose will you find in your dash?

This book is a compilation of personal milestones. Transitions. Losses. Challenges. Wins. I've gone places that were difficult but necessary in order to pull back the curtain, to share my life so far. There were times when I was crying on the inside. Times when things weren't going well at home or weren't what I wished they could be at work. Those times when I've smiled on the outside and said "Good morning" or "Good afternoon" to thousands of people watching—times that I've given it my all when "my all" seemed like more than I could give—those are the times that contain, for me, the biggest lessons, and that's why I'm sharing them with you. They're the most meaningful moments in my dash—so far. The hope is that my experiences will help you in some way. Maybe shine some light on a dark time you're facing or maybe just make you smile. Maybe they'll keep you company as you work your own way through.

Because we all need company. I'm fortunate: I haven't been alone. I have family. I have friends. I have those values that were imprinted on me by my upbringing, daily, and also during those key moments, like seeing my dad on a school stage bellowing out his message about the importance of that dash. For me, this means thinking hard about how I use my microphone. How can I speak the truth from this platform I've been given? How can I make a change? Be a force for good in my community? How can I honour those I cherish most?

How can I be kind?

I want to heap all the joyful, meaningful and generous living I can onto my dash. It takes training, I think, to do that. It takes practice. It takes discipline. It takes faith, in yourself and the people around you. It takes knowing how to get back up and knowing there are people who have your back.

I tell other people's stories for a living. That's what reporters do. We research, collect facts and then create a narrative. But now—I'm telling my own. I hope, in doing so, that I can offer something helpful and meaningful to yours.

Dance, baby, dance

There's a special skill set television show hosts have to have. No matter what's going on behind the scenes, looking fresh-faced, bright-eyed and warm are mandatory requirements. It doesn't matter if you fought with your partner or couldn't sleep the night before: you've got to bring the energy and do so believably.

I have acting chops. I know this because many a day I have sat at that desk, buried what I was really feeling, and belted out a hearty "Good morning, Canada!" or "Today on *The Social!*"

I can fool most people but not those who really know me. My eyes betray me. Lately it's Lainey Lui, one of my co-hosts on *The Social*, who's the first to say, "What's going on with you? Your eyes have that look in them."

That usually leads, when time allows, to a heart-to-heart. To me confessing my inner worries.

What if I'm always alone?

What if my best years are behind me?

Here's the sort of thing Lainey says: "I don't accept that, Marci. Your best years are definitely ahead of you. You're just feeling stuck and have to let some things go. Even let some people go. Get the fresh start you deserve."

Lainey has talked me off a cliff so many times. She's honest and real, and she tells me the truth whether it hurts or not.

Stuck. She's right. Some days I feel like a shadow of myself. I'm moving but not taking the steps I should. I'm not all that I can be. There's a butterfly trying to break free, but the cocoon is layered and feels like cement.

"Thank God you're alive"

I was jammed in the gap between the driver's and front passenger's seats. Jammed, but also cushioned—the seats had prevented me from flying through the windshield. I opened my eyes. I saw glass everywhere. Mangled metal. My friend Dominik, hunched over and bleeding from the head.

He whispered slowly—he was really out of it—"Marci, are you OK?"

I think I answered him. I might have just answered in my head. I was relieved to hear his voice. I thought, *I'm so glad he's alive.*

Then came another voice, a woman's. "Thank God you're alive," she said, an echo of my own thought about Dom. "Help is on the way."

I couldn't see the person talking to me, I couldn't move to look, but a hand appeared. Just a hand. It came through a gap in the wreckage and held mine.

"I'm a nurse," said the voice. Soothing. Kind. "Don't worry," she said. Her name was Linda. "You're not alone."

Sometime after that I heard a paramedic or firefighter saying, "What are you doing here? I just saw you on television this morning."

And so they had. It was early 2003 and I was a news anchor for *Canada AM*. Lloyd and I had been married for only a couple of years and didn't have Blaize yet. My day would have begun at four, when Dom picked me up in an old Caddy with plush seats. Dom was a driver for CTV. He got me to the studio each day at that ungodly hour and back home afterward. In the business, they call that early-morning schedule a "hardship shift." You're assigned a driver, in part, to get there on time. Also to allow you that precious travel time to prepare for the morning mayhem of a daily news show. During the fifteen or so minutes it took for Dom to drive from our townhouse to the CTV studios in Agincourt, just off Highway 401, I would be reading the newspapers that were in the car for me to look through. I'd be scanning the newswires on my phone, emailing a producer, or checking in with a CTV correspondent about a story we were covering. Later, on the way home, the pre-show frenzy over, Dom and I would chat. He had a good fifteen or more years on me and was from Slovenia. He'd tell me about life there. We'd discuss the news, our families, our lives. Sometimes he'd drive me to an afternoon assignment. We might go to lunch. We were friends.

That morning was crisp, bright and cold. A gorgeous day, stunningly beautiful, but the kind of winter day when you'd find black ice on the roads. I finished the show in high spirits. Often, after a morning show, you're exhausted. But I didn't feel tired that day. Was it the brightness, the sunny sky? I was eager to get outside.

First, though, I'd agreed to lead a tour of students through the studios. I'd been looking forward to it, and it was fun. The kids weren't shy: they asked loads of questions. I took them through the newsroom, the editing bays and onto the sets for CTV News Channel and for *Canada AM*. Back then Lloyd Robertson was chief anchor for the national evening news. I showed them the desk where he sat. They said the sets looked smaller in real life than they'd imagined. They were intrigued by the equipment in the editing suites. A couple of editors stopped to chat and explain to the kids what they did on a typical day.

Two things, looking back, were important about me giving that tour on that particular morning. First, I saw everyone before I left the building: co-workers, colleagues working on other shows—many people I wouldn't necessarily run into on a regular morning. Second, because I was at the station later than usual, Dom didn't have to wait for me. We had cab chits we could use, and I'd told him I was perfectly alright to get myself home. He insisted on staying.

Around midday, after the tour, I left the building and walked out to meet Dom. The piercing sunlight caught me off guard. I got into my usual seat in the car: back seat, right-hand side.

I didn't put my seatbelt on, which was normal for me in this car. I don't know why. I guess it was like getting into a cab. Do people put seatbelts on in cabs? It wasn't the right thing to do, but it was my habit.

We were on the highway in the left lane—the fast lane. Suddenly the car in front of us swerved into the middle lane. We understood immediately why it had veered so quickly. A truck had stopped. A huge truck, like a Mack truck. It must have had some trouble and tried to pull over onto the shoulder. But it was too big. Half the truck was sticking out into the fast lane. Our lane. We were headed straight for it.

I thought I was done. I thought, *This is it.* I really did. To go full speed into an object at a standstill—it didn't take a lot of imagination to think, *This is where I meet my end.* I didn't feel angry at all. It was more a feeling of shock. *OK. Wow. This is happening.*

We slammed into the truck.

They used the jaws of life to get us out. Dom's injuries were more serious than mine: he had some internal bleeding. They were worried about his lung. He went to Sunnybrook Hospital. I went to Scarborough General.

Meanwhile, I had asked the paramedic to call my dad. Then Dad called everyone else: my mom, my sister, my work. The newsroom manager at CTV, Karen, was a good friend of mine. She said to him, "What do you mean? I just saw her." He had to repeat to her, gently, "Karen, Marci was in an accident."

And such an accident. A television chopper was covering it because it had blocked the highway. Colleagues of mine on their way for the afternoon shift saw the wreckage on their drive to work. When they arrived, they were horrified to learn that it was us.

My sister, Lorraine, had been taking her youngest daughter, Sari, to a doctor's appointment. After hearing from Dad, they didn't go. Instead, they turned back to pick up her middle daughter from school. Lorraine told me later that Jordy, called down to the office, had skipped in, happy-go-lucky, excited that there was something going on—some reason to get out of class. But she looked at my sister's face and saw something else. My sister said, "Marci's been in an accident." Jordy didn't speak. She went straight to her locker, got her things, ran back, and they were already at the hospital when I arrived. Lloyd was away on business in New York. I didn't see him until that night, but one of his brothers came to the hospital to see if I was OK. A vice-president of CTV News, Joanne MacDonald, took Sari back to work with her so she wouldn't be stuck in the hospital all day—it was a long time for a little kid. So she spent the day at the station with Joanne.

Everybody who came to the hospital saw the wreckage because to get there you had to take the 401. Lorraine had actually driven by it earlier on her way to pick up Sari. She told me she'd thought to herself, *Those people didn't survive.*

Then she'd found out it was me.

But we had, against the odds, it seems, survived. I was discharged from the hospital with a broken rib, and I was deeply bruised. There's not much you can do with a rib. The bruises weren't really visible until a day or two later. Then I looked like someone had treated my legs and upper body like a punching bag.

Because I had to stay home to recover, I was unable to visit Dom at Sunnybrook. I felt terrible the accident had happened after he'd waited around to drive me home. Thankfully, he made a full recovery. The car was demolished. Dom saw it, but I never did. I never wanted to. It wasn't hard getting back on the highway, though, whether in the car with Dom or driving myself. As soon as I went back to work, it was Dom who picked me up. I didn't think twice about it.

I did think, though, and still do, about the fact that we survived. It very easily could have gone the other way. But it wasn't our time. Why not? I felt fortunate to be alive, but I also felt there was a deeper meaning. *There's a reason I'm here. There are some things I still have to do. Maybe,* I thought, *I have a voice that still needs to be heard. There are people to serve. There's a family I need to take care of and be there for.*

I stopped taking life, just waking up in the morning, for granted. It's said that people often say that sort of thing after a big life event, and it's true. I started to use the term "love" harder. I understood that time is a commodity, and I had to make sure I used it to spend time with the people I cared about, to not give away hours that I didn't have. It was a major step, to acknowledge how important that is. I used to say yes to a lot of requests and invitations. *Would I like to host this event? Would I be interested in being part of this group?* Yes, yes, of course, yes. I wanted to help all the people I could help. But after the accident, I began to fine-tune, to think about where I wanted to spend my time. It became women, and it became kids—those two areas became my focal points as far as lending my time, my presence and my voice. I couldn't serve everybody, and it was important to serve the right way. It was a hard lesson.

I also just really appreciated things more. Kindnesses. Right down to the way we use language, how we talk to each other. The whole idea of saying, "See you tomorrow!"

I still think about that sometimes. *Will* I see them tomorrow? Hopefully.

Kindness. Appreciation. On the air after my recovery, I spoke about Linda, the woman who'd thrust her hand through the wreckage to grab mine, who'd said to me, "Thank God you're alive." I had tried to find her. I scoured the directories of nursing associations, everything I could think of. I hoped someone who knew her might hear me mention her on the air. But she had either disappeared or didn't want to be found. In quiet moments, I catch myself wondering, *Was this some sort of other being? Some kind of angel situation?* Your mind goes to those places. You just don't know. I don't know who this woman was. I never found her. If somehow she reads this, I want her to know: I will never forget her kindness.

Kindness. Appreciation. After the accident, for a time, our townhouse looked like a garden. Cards and flowers came from friends, family, from fans all across the country. Bouquets arrived from clusters of colleagues. From CTV executives. From the union that represented technicians and camera operators. It was a small townhouse, and the little island in the kitchen, where the flowers stood, was full. There was no place to use a cutting board to chop a carrot. There were flowers in vases on the floor. Flowers everywhere. Almost every day there would be a fresh delivery.

I hunkered down among all those flowers to heal. The townhouse was narrow and three storeys high. I could barely take the stairs, so I mostly lived on the couch on the first floor, amid all those blossoms and well wishes. Friends visited. A fellow reporter sent me the novel *The Red Tent* and some other books. My dad brought me roti. My mom and my sister cooked.

But my friends and family, my kind visitors, were there during the day. The evenings were a different situation. Lloyd worked at night on the weekends because he owned a nightclub in downtown Toronto. That first Saturday night, a couple of days after the accident, he came downstairs dressed for work, car keys in hand. The whole deal. I thought, *Huh? You can't be going in.*

"Do you have to go?" I asked him. "I don't want to be alone."

"Do I *have* to go?" he repeated. Drawing out the word "have." Punctuating it, to make a point. "No. I don't have to. You're going to be fine," he said. And he walked out the door.

I thought, *Wow.*

Maybe it struck me because I was surrounded by so much kindness from others. I was engulfed in kindness. Except from the quarter that mattered most. I remember feeling so alone.

And then, just putting it away. I didn't even tell my family. I didn't tell anyone I was by myself that night. I was ashamed.

This is what we do, isn't it? We put things away, for when the time is right.

Actually, there were three things I put away after the accident. Three important things. Leaving the station that morning, I had changed into my boots and thrown my shoes into my purse. They were oxblood heels with a closed toe, really cute. The purse was a Louis Vuitton bucket bag, dark brown with a caramel strap, that I had bought myself for my birthday a couple of years earlier.

The bag, with a bloodstain on the strap, and a single shoe were recovered after the crash.

The shoe I put away in the closet with all the others: it's there to this day, the only lone shoe in the mix.

The bloodstained bag I keep on a shelf with the rest of my purse collection. Some people, to commemorate a milestone, promotion or anniversary, buy themselves jewellery or treat themselves to a fancy dinner. Me, I'll buy a purse. Friends and family have bought purses for me for special occasions. So the Louis Vuitton bag is there among all the others.

I held on to these objects and put them away so I would always have that evidence, those reminders, of what had happened—and what had *almost* happened. Of the new lease on life I'd received.

The other thing I put away, though, was that sinking feeling

I had about my still-young marriage, after Lloyd went into work that night. The realization that, surrounded by all these floral gestures of love, I felt abject loneliness.

This is what we do when we're not ready to face reality. We put reality away. We tuck it away in a dark closet, up on a shelf, like a purse or a shoe. You can get stuck in the pattern of putting things away: you shelve them, and you reshelve them. And then one day, the shelf is overburdened. It breaks. And everything just crumbles.

But that crisis, for me, was still a long way off. My shelf sure wasn't empty, but it was holding up.

I don't think I blame myself for putting that doubt about my marriage away. We can waste way too much energy second-guessing the choices we made in the past. I had so much to process after that accident. Maybe we can handle only one turning point in life at a time.

I was grateful to be alive. For the time being, that was quite enough.

"I want a sister"

My sister, Lorraine, was seven years old when I was born, and she says that I am the only thing she ever really asked for, out loud. She's grateful for many things. She has wanted many things. But I was her one actual request: "I asked for a sister," she'll say. "I asked Mom and Dad for you."

It's tempting to think someone should have told her, "Be careful what you ask for. You just might get it." But Lorraine wasn't the kind of big sister who ever found her much-younger sibling annoying or in the way. My own daughter, Blaize, who's seven years older than her brother, Dash, is that kind of sister sometimes: she doesn't always want her brother around. This is natural: we expect it of siblings. Sometimes they need their space. But Lorraine was different. She always included me.

She never left me behind. Her friends knew we were a package deal. She made it clear she wanted me around. She brought me everywhere. She made me feel like I expanded her life, not constrained it.

While we were growing up, Mom was working on her accounting degree, so Lorraine filled in the gaps. She mothered me. She sometimes brought me with her to school on PA days, explaining to her teachers that I was accompanying her for the day. She taught me to take pride in how I look and made sure I dressed well. Out of the earnings from her part-time job, she bought me my first designer sweater and jeans combo: a lilac Ralph Lauren cotton pullover and a turquoise pair of Gloria Vanderbilt jeans. Mostly, though, and by example—how she treated me—she taught me empathy and how to be there for the people you love.

She's my rock. My caregiver, my cheerleader. My first phone call for everything—good or bad or in between. She's the one I go to for solace, advice. When something goes my way, it's Lorraine I want to celebrate with. I tell people that without Lorraine, I don't exist.

One summer, our parents went away to France for a month. (Dad used to teach there in the summers, and this particular year, Mom had gone to join him near the end of his stint, and they stayed on for a holiday.) I was thirteen, my sister twenty. Our parents had left money, and Lorraine was in charge of me. To Lorraine—she's crazy, she's nuts—that meant, whatever she and her friends were doing, I was doing. So she gave me her U of T ID and snuck me into clubs. For a month, it seemed, we had the run of the city. We still call it *That* Summer.

Her sixtieth birthday is not that far off. That scares me a little. She's always been the one who seems invincible—a superhero. But now, all of a sudden, wow. Mortality. I think: thank God for Lorraine, and thank God she asked for me to be born.

I think: slow down, time, there's still so much to do.

I have lived, since childhood, feeling in some way as if I was summoned here, into this life, by my sister—by her telling my parents she wanted a sister; she *needed* one. And when you are called to this world by a person like Lorraine, you're born with a built-in purpose. You have a thing or two to live up to.

What a joy and a gift it is, to try and to keep trying, with her by my side.

Hockey girl

I grew up in Toronto, but my dad's hockey team of choice—maybe because he studied and speaks French?—was the Montreal Canadiens. As a girl I'd watch the games with him. One year, when I was eight or nine years old, I thought it would be neat to play hockey. But there was no hockey for girls in my area. Just ringette.

I was not too excited about ringette.

So what did my dad do? He carefully read the regulations, didn't see any specific rule against it, and signed me up for a boys' team. House league. We bought all the gear, and with the helmet on, I don't think anybody could really tell the difference. I was so young. He drove me to Glen Watford Arena in Scarborough for games and practices.

I wasn't any good. Finding my balance and my footing didn't come naturally. Maybe the equipment didn't fit right because it wasn't made for girls? I don't know. I still have scars on my knees from the pads that chafed my skin. But I loved playing. I wasn't thinking that I was a girl and the rest of the players were boys. I was just thrilled to be on the ice, to have all the equipment. I liked the excitement: to push that puck.

I thought my dad rocked. I wanted to play hockey and he didn't say, "Ringette is where you're meant to be." He didn't let my gender stop me.

Granny

I met one of my closest friends in grade two. Our family had just moved to Scarborough, and I was the new kid at school. Debbie, a kind heart if there ever was one, befriended me right away and invited me to her house for lunch one day. She lived across the street from our school. My house was a couple of blocks away. My parents both worked full-time, so going home for lunch wasn't an option. But Deb's grandmother was home, and she told my parents it would be no problem for me to have lunch at the house, too.

Thus began one of my fondest childhood memories. Deb, Granny and I had a routine. Granny loved her "stories," as she called them. Her favourite was *The Young and the Restless*, known to 1980s soap aficionados as *Y&R*. Deb and I would race to her house as soon as the lunch bell rang. Granny was there to greet us. While munching on our meals—rice and peas, chicken curry, the most delicious oxtail stew, fried dumplings, or the best ackee and saltfish ever—the three of us would be glued to the TV.

Deb and I were seven years old. OK, maybe it wasn't exactly appropriate viewing for us, but it was our thing with Granny, and I loved it. What would happen next with Victor and Nikki? Would Mrs. Chancellor realize that she was eating poisoned chocolates? Who would Ashley end up with? We were absolutely entranced.

Deb, now a nurse living in Texas, has always been as kind as her grandmother. She and I have stayed close through the years. While in university, we often spent spring break together travelling to the Caribbean or the southern US. She is also a fabulous concert partner. We've crossed the border to attend some great concerts in Buffalo, New York: Bobby Brown, Luther Vandross, Lionel Richie. I've visited her in Texas, and we catch up whenever she comes to Toronto. Our lasting friendship reminds me of the importance of the connections we make as kids, those friends whose history with us goes all the way back to the days when we were learning how to move through the world, how to be ourselves and be with other people at the same time. It also makes me think about how sometimes when you make a friend, you get the extra benefit of knowing the important people in their lives. When you're a kid, the home of your friend, even if it's just around the corner, is like a whole different country from your own.

Granny passed away some years ago. Deb said that even in her last years of life she was still talking about *The Young and the Restless*. Granny had treated me like I was one of her own. She was generous and kind. And I still remember the glorious taste of her oxtail stew.

A personality for television

Now and then in the hallway at work I run into Stacie Spalding, a television director in the building. As Stacie and I happily say hi to each other, a person passing by might guess right away that we're more than colleagues—we're friends. Old friends. What they'd never guess, though, is the true significance of that friendship. Stacie is a direct link back to my first experience of being on television, an experience that in some ways defined my childhood and shaped who I am today.

For six years while we were growing up, Stacie and I spent every Saturday together as cast members on the children's TV show *Circle Square*. You can even find a photo of us together online from back then: Stacie with her red hair pulled back and me with my tall 1980s hair, both of us dressed in shirts buttoned up to our necks (hers with a collar, mine tied with a bow). When I joined *Circle Square* during a cast changeover in 1979, Stacie and I started together. In fact, her father, John Spalding, was the director, and her mom, Maggie, was one of the show's producers. To me, however, being on TV was a whole new world. Looking back, it's almost surprising it became part of my life at all.

Here's how it happened. I've mentioned that I sometimes spent time at my dad's school on my PA days and I'd hang around the office. I wasn't shy. I was precocious. Many of the teachers got to know me. One of them had a child who'd acted in commercials. She told my dad one day she thought I had a personality for television. And what's more, she knew of an open audition being held for a children's show. She gave him the details, and that evening at home he talked it over with my mom and me.

I found the idea of television and of being with other kids exciting. Why not try?

That teacher had pegged me: though she couldn't have known this, at my own school, I nearly always had some little performance thing going on. I was in school plays. My friends and I would make up dances to songs like Michael Jackson's "Dancing Machine." We'd actually gather classes together to watch us, like it was an assembly. I have no idea why the teachers would go along with us. It was a small public school, and they allowed us to do that.

I need to stop here and reflect. There I was, ten years old, with a mother who was studying to become an accountant and a principal father who had studied at Harvard. Their message to me and my sister had always been to put our studies first. They weren't into extracurricular activities like sports and clubs. Piano lessons, which I hated, were the exception: I was told I had to have an instrument. I used to tell my mom my instrument was my voice. Yet they considered this opportunity, they talked it over with me, they saw how keen I was, and they gave me permission. They said I could do the audition.

I think, in hindsight, that their choice hinged on the show being Christian in its messaging. It was produced by Crossroads Christian Communications, the same company that made *100 Huntley Street*, and it was filmed in the same studio. My parents' thinking must have been that at least I wouldn't be corrupted!

Being who they were, they could easily have said no. They didn't. But they must not have understood fully what I—what we—were getting into when they surprised me with that "yes."

My dad drove me to a big church on Bloor Street in downtown Toronto for the audition. There must have been a hundred kids inside. Dad filled out some information sheets and we waited for my name to be called. For some reason, I wasn't nervous. The audition consisted of three stations. I was first asked to do what's called a responsive reading, where someone reads a line from a script and you read the next line. Then I performed a scene with another kid. The last thing was to sing a song. I had prepared for this: being able to sing was a prerequisite for the show, which contained a lot of original music. I performed "Amazing Grace," which was my favourite song. I knew it from church. I loved the words and the song's simplicity.

A week later, I was called for a second round. More script readings. A kind of interview, with questions about what sort of things I liked to do, did I have any siblings, and so on.

Another week of waiting, and then I was offered a role. I accepted and remained a cast member until 1985. By then, I was sixteen. Who knew, when the chance of that audition came up, that *Circle Square* would basically take up my whole childhood and start me on the path that led to where I am today? For six years, every Saturday morning, my dad woke me up at four thirty to drive me to 100 Huntley Street. All the kids had our makeup and hair done and were on-set for six thirty for our first rehearsal. There were ten kids in the cast, and we'd shoot all day, till three or four o'clock. It was my life, my routine: some kids went out to play or did gymnastics on a Saturday morning. I got a ride downtown and reported to the set at dawn.

Circle Square was like a kids' variety show with a different theme each week. We had a clubhouse where all the kids hung out after school. We had puppets named Gert and Egbert. A kid would come in and say hi to everyone, and Egbert would say, "Marci, what's wrong? You look sad." And I'd say, "I was at school. Some kids were smoking. I didn't want to. They made fun of me." He'd say, "Why don't you go tell Durk? He'll know what to do." Durk was the school janitor (he had a puppet friend, too, named Vince). So we'd go talk to Durk, and he'd say, "You know, I remember a story that sounds a lot like this one. Once upon a time…" And then we would play these taped episodes that involved kids dealing with the problem the kid had that day—what to do, how to deal with certain situations. Afterward, the kid would feel better and go back to the club-house. There'd be songs, and we'd read letters from a mailbag.

For my first couple of months on the show, I felt like a fish out of water. Many of the other cast members had experience. They'd done commercials, plays or other productions. One boy, Jason, sang the TV jingle for Mr. Christie's cookies. In comparison, I was completely green.

But I had a good memory. I was comfortable in front of the camera. What's more, everybody was so warm and helpful. I quickly felt at home. I've always been a reader, and I really liked the idea of going through the scripts. They were mailed to us in white envelopes, maybe a couple of weeks of episodes at a time. Sometimes I'd go through them with my parents. We'd read them and I'd practise my lines.

I enjoyed those Saturdays on-set so much. I was amazed by and loved learning the details of producing a television show. I got to see and study how camera shots were taken and how a set was marked for where we had to sit. I learned about camera angles, looking from camera one to camera two, and working with a floor director.

It was like a job. Not only did we spend Saturdays taping, we also had music rehearsals during the week, and over the years recorded two albums of songs from the show. So we'd be in the studios laying down tracks on weeknights. But it gave me so much. The first building block of my work ethic happened on that set. Rehearsals. Memorizing lines. Hitting the right marks.

Being on that show trained my brain. I can pick things up and process information very quickly. I had it down at ten years old.

It was more than that, though—what I learned from the show extended into my life. The commitment taught me to be organized: I became skilled in budgeting my time, making sure my school work didn't suffer; I grew disciplined about having a call time, knowing I could never be late. There were things I had to forego. I ran a bit of track in high school, but I couldn't commit to much. I was doing the show.

I think, too, that the show's themes themselves influenced me. They were reminders. Lessons. You can't study something and not have it permeate your belief system. I was studying those scripts, learning the lines, but also learning the morals and the character types that were part of all that. The scenarios had to do with not being afraid to be your own person, how to have the courage to speak up, to do the right thing, not go with the crowd. Because it was a Christian show, the message was clear: You don't need to meld in; you can lead. Looking back, I can see that we did some pretty interesting things. We went places. There was a show about shoplifting. Another one about gossip. Overcoming fear. As the cast members got older, the script writer, Jana Lyn Rutledge, wrote the stories to fit our ages—to address the kinds of issues we'd be dealing with. Like smoking and drinking. So there we'd be, puffing away on cigarettes for a scene. I had never even smoked outside the show!

We shot the taped segments on location, in different parts of Ontario and even went to Jamaica. When we were away, Stacie and I would often room together. We became really close. I remember confiding to her once that I felt out of place. I had been thinking I was overweight—I was already struggling, at that young age, with the idea of my appearance on a television screen. I remember her saying, "You look great. You have to remember to love yourself more." She was full of conviction and inspiration. When I didn't feel great, she came through. She was my own little cheering squad.

I didn't realize it at the time, but *Circle Square* prepared me for my entire career. I don't mean just about television and learning how to do that. I mean doing it with other kids, and those kids, because we spent so much time together, turning into a kind of family. In the end, what I got from that show was a six-year-long lesson in how to do your part and lift other people up in the process. We were our own tribe.

So, these days, when I see Stacie in the hall at work and we smile, there's a whole lot of history behind our smiles—a childhood's worth of wisdom picked up between the lines of the scripts we learned together on that old *Circle Square* set.

The view from Jamaica

We were settling into our seats on an Air Jamaica flight—the cast and crew of *Circle Square*. It was an international program, syndicated to television stations not just across Canada, but also in the US and Jamaica. We often filmed on location during the summer at different sites in Ontario; in winter, we'd go down to the West Indies for a week, maybe two. The company that owned the show, Crossroads Christian Communications, had a person on staff to help us with our school work. My parents were on board so long as I kept up my grades. So there I was, ten years old and going to stay at the exclusive Half Moon resort in Montego Bay.

I hadn't travelled extensively. My paternal grandparents lived in New York, and we'd sometimes go visit them. We'd gone on road trips to Ottawa and Quebec. But to get on a plane and go to Jamaica—without my parents in tow—was a whole different situation. I wasn't scared. I'd been on a plane before. But to be on one with just my friends: let me tell you, this was exciting.

Circle Square wasn't exactly prime-time television. In Canada, we had a modest, loyal audience. I suspect many people were vaguely aware the show existed, but they'd never watched it. Kids might land on it by accident while flipping through channels looking for cartoons on a Saturday morning. In Jamaica, it was a different story. There were two TV channels, and *Circle Square* was on one of them. So us coming down to film on location was a big deal. We were announced on the plane. People met us at the airport. They sang as we disembarked. Photographers snapped pictures. We gave interviews. There was a write-up in the local newspaper. It was as if actual celebrities had landed.

But it wasn't the celebrity treatment during those trips that affected me most. It wasn't the place we stayed: I didn't grasp, at that age, how grand and exclusive it was. It wasn't the taping we did in the streets, on golf courses or in public gardens. It wasn't even the humanitarian work we did, which included visits to orphanages and singing for the children who lived in them. It was Jamaica itself: being in that country and experiencing a society and a culture that was so different from the one back home in Canada.

It may partly have been the different climate, but I was struck by how the people there were remarkably, genuinely warm: their smiles, handshakes and welcome. Here at home, people just go about their business. We live in silos. But there, it's "How can we help you?" "You should really see this place" and "Have you tried this food? Because you really need to!"

Jamaica is a nation of storytellers. People will sit with you and take the time to tell you about their relatives, the land, their background, their home. It's my kind of place because I love to ask other people about their lives. I love to hear their stories. If you're in the back of a cab, or buying some food, or—as we did while there—hanging out at the orphanage, my instinct is to say, "Tell me who you are." In Jamaica, no one balks at your curiosity. They don't think it's crazy. They smile. They enjoy the question. And they answer you. In full.

During my years with *Circle Square*, we travelled to Jamaica three times, maybe four. That's all. But it was enough to make that country my comfort zone: the place I long to go when I need to recalibrate, recharge or heal. I connected with Jamaica—with the people and with the land. I felt very much at home there. When I was in university, my friend Debbie, whose background is Jamaican, would go down with me on spring break. My good friend Donovan Bailey, the retired sprinter and Canadian Olympic legend, who partly grew up in Ontario and partly in Jamaica, lives there half the time. We chat on the phone sometimes: here, it's snowing outside my window, while he is poolside in the tropics. Of course he taunts me; he lords it over me. But we get serious, too. We talk about that land, how special it is, the belief that the land can cure you—of anything from illness to heartache. The gift of being able to climb a mango tree, grab a mango and dice it up.

We also talk about what it means to us and what it meant to us as children, to spend time in a society so obviously led and run by Black people. The Jamaican prime minister is Black. Doctors, teachers and lawyers are Black. These people are in positions of responsibility. They're running things. Though we have a diverse population in Canada, and Black people do indeed rise to positions of prominence and influence, to see Black Canadians in positions of leadership here is still not the norm. So to travel to Jamaica as a young Black person from Canada and find myself surrounded by Black excellence; to suddenly be in a place where Black excellence is ordinary and expected; to spend time in a society where daily news featuring Black people isn't dominated by stories of violence, hardship and struggle—that was powerful. It was transformative. It opened my eyes to the possibility that things could be dramatically different from what I saw around me back home, and that, in some very particular ways, they should be.

No maid service

I was twelve and had been performing on *Circle Square* for two years. The scripts arriving weekly in the mail had become part of our family routine. Because we did on-location shoots during the summer, we'd sometimes receive a very fat envelope containing the scripts for ten or fifteen segments. One evening, my dad and I were reading through a heap together. I had my favourite yellow highlighter in my hand for marking my lines. Suddenly Dad grabbed the pages right out of my hand and marched into the other room, where my mom was. A few moments passed. He must have given Mom the pages to read, for all at once I heard her declare, "My daughter will not play a maid!"

Next thing I knew, Dad was on the phone to the show's

producer, explaining that he and my mother had serious issues with the part I'd been assigned. He said their daughter would absolutely not play the part of a maid in a fictional white household. It hadn't been an intentional slight or slur, but in some sense that was as bad or worse than a deliberate, malicious act of racism: that it would simply seem natural for the show's creators to slot the Black girl into the role of the maid lifted the lid on the kind of underlying, subconscious racism that people of colour still encounter all the time. These days it would be called a micro-aggression, but there's nothing small about it. They heard what my father had to say and resolved the issue quickly. The producer assigned another child, Stacie, to the role, and I wasn't in that drama.

Decades later, I remember that night as if it were yesterday. The lesson was quick and stark and indelible. My parents had taught me through their actions to speak up. To not accept racism in any form. Their example has guided me throughout my life and given me the conviction to use my voice, even in the face of opposition. Even when it's uncomfortable, exhausting or awkward. It shouldn't have been their job, in that moment, to educate the showrunners of *Circle Square*. But they had no choice. So they sent the writer and producer a message they wouldn't likely forget: now you know better, so do better.

The way I see it, my parents seeded change—perhaps even a newfound empathy—in at least two hearts that night. And planted a firm principle in mine.

Thirteen (part one)

It was a Monday morning. Breakfast. Gearing up for school. The usual start-of-the-week routine. I normally caught the bus. But that day, Dad offered to drive me to school. That in itself was odd. I figured something was up.

We lived in Scarborough in what would now be called a "starter" home. Plans were afoot for us to find a place that was a little bit larger. We'd looked at a house that weekend in a development by Heathwood Homes, a big-name developer in the area. If you can fall for a house, I'd fallen for that one. Hard.

In my child's mind, that house was just so fancy. It was spacious and also had a big backyard. But the real kicker? It had this pretty bay window. I could see myself sitting there, curled up in the window, reading a book, looking out onto the garden. I could envision every perfect detail.

That morning, getting in the car with Dad, I was still thinking of the house, imagining us moving there. But I'd figured right: something was up. He could hardly get the words out. "Your mom and I are going to split up," he said. He was so upset he was crying. "We're going to sell the house — but we won't be moving into a new one together." I was shocked. Numb.

He didn't give any reasons. He didn't say a lot. For a man who was usually so eloquent, all he could manage was "You know I'm your dad and I'll always be here for you. That will never change."

As the news sank in, I realized maybe I shouldn't have been surprised. My parents had never seemed close. They weren't affectionate. Conversation was minimal. Their silence told the story. But at the same time, when a family's breaking up, a family's breaking up. The dysfunction was there, but it was *our* dysfunction. All of a sudden it was just crumbling. It was hard to take.

I wonder now if that family house-hunting project was what finally did it: maybe Dad, or both Mom *and* Dad, realized they couldn't start over together in a new place. Their life together would actually come to an end in the so-called "starter" home. I don't remember my mom talking with me about what was happening. I think she was in self-preservation mode: we had to find a new home, a place to live. She had to stay focused on that; she couldn't handle one more thing. She was struggling just to take care of herself.

Luckily, I had my sister. Lorraine and I would live with my mom, and Dad would find a place close by. We knew that as long as she and I were together, we'd be fine.

My love language and my mom

After my parents separated, we lived—my sister, our mom and I—in a split-level suburban house in Scarborough. Although there was a front door, people usually came in through the side. There was a pantry on that level, and a few steps down was the basement, which had a family room. Up a level was the more formal living room, with a French provincial couch and chairs, and a door that led to the backyard. To the right of that was my room. I had a view of my mom's hydrangea and rose bushes and her fruit trees. We had apple and pear trees and strawberry bushes. It was a big, lush yard. I think Mom created a space back there that reminded her of Trinidad.

Up another couple of steps from my room was the kitchen and a large dining room. Mom loved what she called well-made furniture. We had a heavy wooden table with an extra leaf and an equally weighty hutch for the good dishes. A proper table cloth. Crystal. Cutlery. Up another level was my mom's bedroom, my sister's bedroom and the spare room.

In later years that room became Mom's sewing room, spilling over with fabrics. Mom was a skilled seamstress. But for a time, when I was sixteen, this was where Alison stayed.

According to author Gary Chapman, there are five "love languages": quality time, physical touch, acts of service, words of affirmation, and gift-giving. Chapman argues that people in a romantic relationship relate to their partners primarily through one of these languages. The idea of having a "love language" resonates with me, but I take a little licence and extend it — well beyond the limits of those five languages as defined by Chapman and also beyond the confines of romance. I believe a person's love language can take any number of forms; I also think that it rules the way we relate to all the people in our lives that we care about — family, friends, even colleagues — not just a life partner.

My own love language is kindness. That's what attracts me to people. It's what I try to model for my kids: heart first. Kindness first. What are you doing for other people? What are your plans in that vein? I love when I meet a heart that operates on kindness because I do think it's rare. And I would know one anywhere because it's the kind of heart I saw in action, up close and personal, when I was growing up.

My mother was unbelievably kind and generous, always opening her door to others. She and I didn't see eye to eye on everything when I was younger. We still don't. Her views are more conservative than mine, so we don't always agree on social issues. And as an accountant, she was always very much about living within your means and respecting your limits. I did not like limits; I wanted to smash them. I confess, I still do.

But when I was sixteen and my ex-boyfriend called regarding a crisis in his own family, I knew that I could turn to Mom for help. He knew it, too, which was why he called.

Some background. First of all, my boyfriend had become my ex because he'd dumped me in order to go out with one of my friends. No joke. So the end of our relationship was one of my first experiences with the ways that love and betrayal can wrench your heart.

Later, one of his cousins, a girl named Alison who was several years older than I was, lived with him and his family. She had become pregnant. Unfortunately, my ex's mom had no interest in Alison's circumstances, and she was no longer welcome in their house. She was going to be kicked out.

He was worried. Where would she go? He didn't know what to do or who to call. Then he thought of us. We had a spare room. And Mom was known for taking people in. This was partly through the church, which was community focused. There were a couple of pastors who knew that people in need were welcome at our house for a few months. It wasn't ever a family, just single people down on their luck. In between jobs, facing some unforeseen transition, that kind of thing. Once, a woman in her late fifties, a former teacher suffering financial hardship, stayed with us. Another time, it was a woman in her twenties who had trouble at home: she came to us until she could find her own place to live.

So even after all the drama and ugliness of our breakup, my ex knew that it was safe to call me and say, "You're a good person. Your family are good people. Can Alison stay with you? Just until she and her boyfriend figure things out?"

And likewise, I knew that it was safe to go to my mom—who was pretty strict and held to pretty traditional Christian values—about this pregnant young woman and say, "Listen, Mom, she's going to be kicked out. What do you think of her staying with us?" Mom didn't hesitate.

Though Alison had been living with my ex-boyfriend's family, I hardly knew her before she came to stay with us. But she fit in so well; she became like a long-lost sister. My actual sister was older: she had her licence, and we had a vehicle. We were mobile. Sometimes, at eleven o'clock on a Saturday night, we three would jump in the car and drive downtown. I'd rush to the front seat and say, "Get in the back, Alison!" And she'd say, "No respect at all." We'd head to a place called Piece of Cake, where the cake slices were decadent and unbelievably expensive. Or we'd go to this divey place at Dundas and Bay that we called Chicken in a Pot after one of the menu items. It was their signature dish: chicken with ginger, scallions and soy sauce in a crock pot. It was delish. That was a really good time in life.

Now Alison has a son and two daughters, and my sister is godparent to her son. We're very close. She remains like family. Our relationship can be traced directly back to an act of kindness, to my mother and the kind of person she is, and the kind of person she taught me to be.

Out for dinner with my mom and sister.

Rye High locker mate (and diversity)

hen I was ready to graduate from high school and apply to university, we had to rank our three top choices on the application form. I wrote down one. Only one. And Ryerson was it. I wanted to get into the Radio and Television Arts program there. I had worked with several people on *Circle Square* who'd studied at Ryerson, including the director, whose day job was director of CBC Sports. That was the program they did: RTA. That was the one I was going to do, too. These were the footsteps I wanted to walk in.

I had the marks—I was a good student. But thank God I got in. I hadn't told my parents I'd applied to only one school. And I had no Plan B.

I was beyond excited when I received my acceptance. I do remember hearing my dad explain it to people and realizing that for him, who had studied at U of T and at Harvard, Ryerson might seem like a step down. He would say: she acted in a TV show for kids, she wants to work in television, and Ryerson is the best when it comes to that.

He was right—it is. But Ryerson also has a nickname: Rye High. The name fits for a reason. It was very much a commuter school, and at the time, it had no student residences, like most universities do, only a student co-op just off campus. And as in high school, the hallways were lined with lockers, and in September, at the start of the school year, each student was assigned a locker. However, in my year, there weren't enough to go around. I had to share my locker with a guy named Dwight. Dwight Drummond. He asked me where I was from. I said Scarborough, and he kind of looked me up and down. He said I looked like I was fresh off *The Cosby Show*. Clair Huxtable. Tidy, neat. It wasn't a compliment. Whereas Dwight had this tough-guy thing going on. He was from Jane and Finch. I thought he was a little full of it.

Ryerson may have been known as Rye High, but it was no walk in the park. And when it came to workload and expectations, it was leagues away from high school. Our professors were working industry professionals who taught and expected professional-quality work from their students. I remember one professor, Jerry Good, who said to us "Half of you won't be here at graduation." That was day one. "This is not easy. This is the best program in the country. It's going to push you. It's not for the faint of heart."

I felt the truth of those words in radio, for a start. Though I could write good copy and do voice very well, I was terrible

at the technical side: working the boards. There was this one
test where we had to put a three-minute show together. It was
an absolute disaster. I remember being on the mic and saying,
"We're having technical difficulties right now." I barely passed.
I think they gave me fifty percent because at least I tried.

Dwight and I hadn't much liked each other from the get-go.
But as the days and months passed and we shared not just a
locker but classes, we gradually had more time for each other.
We saw each other work and—my technical performance in
radio aside—began to respect each other. It evolved into friendship. As two of a handful of Black students in our year, we supported each other. We looked at the faces around us and knew it
was going to be harder for us to build a career: the statistics were
against us. We studied together. Reminded each other of dead-
lines, assignments, what we had to get done. We pushed each
other. He was the reason I got through things. And he would
later say he would not have graduated if not for me.

Having professors who worked in the industry was an incredible gift. The person at the front of the room talking to us was
already *there*, where we wanted to be. They could share their
insights about what it was like outside school, doing this stuff in
the real world. And they were telling us we had the wherewithal
to get there, too. It's part of the reason I still love the school. It
really prepares people well.

Dwight and I are perfect examples. We graduated during a
recession, the first time the profs in RTA had ever had to warn
their students it might be tough to find a job after earning their
degrees. We both found work, though our early careers were
not without their ups and downs (more on that later). I started

out at CHCH-TV in Hamilton, while Dwight worked for City TV, a media property literally built on Ryerson grads.

Dwight is now a news anchor for CBC Television. We remain the best of friends. He has been in my life for the big decisions, the big changes. He's always been a fighter, going against the grain. He's always talked about things in a true way. I remember his first documentary at school. He called it *Don't Believe the Hype*. He used the Public Enemy song. It was about his community, the Jane and Finch area, how it was misrepresented in news reports and how the good side of the community was never shown. That was his whole thing: this is where I'm from. When someone says "Jane and Finch," you think crime-riddled, you think drugs, yet this is the community that supported him, that helped him get where he is. He remains proud of where he's from, and he's an icon in that area. The man walks on water anywhere in the west end because of what he's accomplished and how he's never forgotten where he's from. There isn't a school invitation that he won't accept. We've gone back to schools and spoken together to kids, talked about our journeys, our work lives, our families, all of that. All this culminated in an idea to create a scholarship in our names at Ryerson. The Marci Ien and Dwight Drummond Award, established in 2015, grants $2,000 each year to a student from a disadvantaged community to put toward their schooling.

I remain involved with Ryerson in other ways, too. I believe so strongly in the value of the institution. Five years ago, I was asked to sit on the school's board of governors. I jumped at the chance even though it meant giving up my role as a visiting professor, coming into classes as a guest speaker a couple of times a month. As a member of the executive committee, I now take part in decision making for the university. And I'm so excited and proud of what's going on.

After my experience as one of the few students of colour in my program thirty-odd years ago, I can confidently say that diversity is now the strength of that school: it's a huge thing on the agenda, and at the core of every decision that gets made, because the people there are such proponents. The chancellor is an Asian woman. The president is a Muslim man. There's an office for diversity that's run by a Black woman. There's a major Indigenous component to both programming and governance. Because the board members have lived such different and interesting lives, the perspectives and viewpoints that come into our discussions make it a very special decision-making group to be a part of.

I think the adolescent Marci who put Ryerson down as her sole option on her university application would be overjoyed to see me sitting around that table now. I also think that, in not bothering to apply anywhere else, she had entirely the right idea. She knew just what she was doing.

Less is more

It was a local fire. Nobody had perished. But we needed to cover it. We needed footage, interviews. A report.

I was a relative newbie at CHCH-TV, otherwise known as Channel 11, in Hamilton. I'd gotten the job during my third and final year at Ryerson. (Now a university, back then Ryerson Polytechnic Institute was a hybrid institution that handed out the equivalent of both college diplomas and degrees. My program, RTA, offered an applied arts degree.) A friend and fellow student had started working at Channel 11 as a weekend writer. She'd told me, "Marci, it's not that bad, going into Hamilton." It was a nine-to-six shift, writing voiceovers for the six o'clock newscast, helping to line up the show, working with the assignment editor.

It was a small shop but big enough that you could learn. Small in the news business can be great for someone just getting their feet wet: if someone called in sick, you'd be doing another job real fast. And that's what happened that weekend of the fire. We were short-staffed. My assignment editor said, "Hey, do you want to go and get some video with a cameraperson and maybe do a story on this?" I jumped at the chance.

There was maybe a couple of thousand dollars' worth of damage. No one had been hurt. I don't remember there being enough pictures to tell the story. I remember the two clips: the people who lived there, the neighbour who'd smelled the smoke. The story ended with a shot of me in a field with this lone police car, probably looking far too nervous, talking about this fire—for way too long. It was drawn out, and it was boring.

Television is more about pictures and less about the talking head. I'd done the exact opposite. It should have had more visuals and less of my voice—and much less of me. Just a voice-over: pictures with my voice in the background, telling the story.

But that was one of the earliest assignments of my career. I was still learning about story structure. You can learn all the things you hear in class, but until you're really doing it, it doesn't start to come together the way it should.

Fast-forward a few years. I was still working for CHCH-TV and had begun filling in at Queen's Park in Toronto for Bob Ireland, the bureau chief at the Ontario legislature, who was having some health problems. It was election season, and things were coming to a head. I was asked to do a report about the coming fiscal changes in the province and how different things would be under the new Conservative government led by incoming premier Mike Harris.

It was a fall day. I was standing at Queen's Park. I was looking authoritative. There were huge maple trees on the property. They were turning colour. I remember this magnificent red-to-gold situation going on. The piece was well written. It was concise, and I closed with something simple like "Change is in the air." A few pointed words and that was it. Then this sweeping shot of those changing leaves filled the screen.

When I got back to the station, I received a note from my news director, John Best. The gist of it was this: *Thank you. That was a great story. Thank you for working so hard. You've improved vastly.*

I'd improved—*vastly*. I had learned through experience that you don't have to fill every single second of your report with your voice. This is television. It's visual. You can let the story breathe. Less is more.

I began to fill in more and more at Queen's Park and, eventually, when Bob retired, I was hired to take his place. With a few years of hard work and hard-won lessons, I'd gone from a student writing weekend copy to *Marci Ien, reporting live from Queen's Park.* That was *my* gig now.

The power of "no"

L anding the Queen's Park job hadn't been a straight road, pothole-free. Early on, when I wasn't long out of Ryerson and still just a part-time news writer at Channel 11 on the weekends, I worked in retail to pay the bills. I had a sales job in a clothing shop in a mall, a Tristan & America store, the same gig I'd held down to help put myself through school.

What I wanted more than anything, though, was to be a reporter. When I had the chance amid those two jobs I was juggling, I kept my eyes open. I looked for opportunities. Job postings. Internships. Calls for applications. I even sent in applications when there was no job posting. On one such occasion, I applied to the local CTV station and was called in for an interview. That was good news: I'd passed the first hurdle.

To get a reporting job on TV you need to provide a tape show-ing clips of yourself at work: on-air, doing interviews, wrapping up a story. Reporting. When I went into the station, the man conducting the interview reviewed my tape. It is nerve-racking, let me tell you, knowing someone is watching you with a really critical eye, assessing your performance—especially if that some-one holds your future in their hands.

When he finished, he told me my work was fine. I just didn't have the "it" factor they were looking for.

At the time, I had a smile plastered on my face, but I was dying on the inside. I was thinking, *This man has been in the industry a long time and he's telling me I don't have what it takes to be successful. Is he right?*

I walked out of his office crushed.

I went and sat in my car, running through what had hap-pened over the past thirty minutes. I talked myself through it, and I kept talking until I could say to myself, *He's wrong. You know he's wrong.*

He told me point-blank that I lacked something fundamen-tal, some unnamed quality required to succeed in this business: the "it" factor. I thought it over, and I took his critique for what it was: a poor explanation for his "no." It wasn't the whole story. And it wasn't going to be my story.

"No" is a powerful word. His "no" forced me to examine myself, my dreams. To ask myself whether I was willing to work even harder until I got where I wanted to be. Do what I needed to do to hone my craft.

I said "yes" to myself that day. I still have self-doubt. I still hear that man's "no" in my head. It has played back in my mind so many times in my career—but the truth is, it's also helped me. It's spurred me to do better because somebody told me I couldn't. Because I was determined to prove him wrong.

Newsroom
(and classroom) calling

I said it wasn't smooth sailing, right? That I didn't go straight from writing news on the weekends to the press gallery at Queen's Park?

Because I sure didn't.

CHCH-TV, like many TV stations, was a union shop. Before I landed the job at Queen's Park, I was, for a time, a not-quite-full-time general assignment reporter. Being the newest hire, whenever there were cutbacks—and there were—I was the first person to be laid off. They always tried to bring me back as soon as possible, which was nice, but even when I had the job, I couldn't count on it. It wasn't stable.

It was a hard time for me. During one of my layoffs, my dad began sharing his worries about the industry I'd chosen. Maybe it wasn't feasible to make a go of it in television. He knew that, as far as a career choice, education had been a close second for me. We talked it over. Maybe I should forget the whole journalism thing. Maybe I should teach.

I applied to something called the Teacher Apprenticeship Program (TAP). It was a two-year deal: For the first year, you would be placed in a school and complete an apprenticeship under a senior teacher. The second year, you were admitted into the faculty of education at the University of Toronto.

I got accepted and was sent to Pierre Laporte, a middle school in Toronto's west end, where I was paired with a veteran teacher. I would sit in her class and observe; I'd help the students with their work; and I'd teach classes myself, under her supervision, in any core subject: math, English, history and so on. She'd assess my interactions with the kids, my lesson plans and how I managed the classroom.

It was quite a feat just to juggle it all. Honestly, these are twelve- and thirteen-year-olds, and you're standing at the front of the classroom with your plan—just to get their attention was an accomplishment. I gave a lesson once on sentence structure: subject and predicate, all that stuff. Bor-ing. At least, it could be. I was explaining the use of "I" and "me": "Mom taught John and me" rather than "Mom taught John and I." I taught them to split the sentences up, to take the middle part out: Which would you say, "Mom taught I" or "Mom taught me"? It was a simple trick that made sense, that they could use to help them remember, and I could see it dawning on them. I'd learned to recognize that look in their eyes when they got it, when what you were saying was sinking in. I remembered watching my dad speaking to his students and seeing their faces and thinking, OK, *he's got them.*

The several months of my teaching apprenticeship were gruelling. Not because of the teaching itself, but because at the same time, to stay afloat, I also worked as a manager in a retail store. My schedule ran as follows: I spent every day from 8:30 a.m. to noon in the classroom. Then I got into my second-hand Hyundai Pony—it was bright red and had these louvres on the back—and drove north to Newmarket, where I managed the Tristan & America location at the Upper Canada Mall from 1 p.m. to 9 p.m. Then I drove home. I'd sometimes have lessons to plan for class in the morning. The next day, I did it all again.

I was working around the clock. It felt like I was always on the highway. My Pony logged thousands of kilometres. It was crazy. Then, at last, the apprenticeship finished. I was two weeks away from starting my education degree at U of T, and I got a call from the news director at Channel 11, John Best. He told me Bob Ireland, the bureau chief at Queen's Park—the reporter I had often filled in for—was retiring. He was offering me Bob's job.

Whoa. What now? I didn't know what to do. Do I go to teachers' college? Or do I take this job? What if I withdraw from teachers' college, go back to the station and, holy smokes, get laid off again in six months? I phoned the registrar and asked if I could defer my position in the program. Just in case. She said, "Absolutely not. There's a waiting list. If you're not going to take the position, I have to offer it to somebody else. Either you want this or you don't."

She gave me forty-eight hours. I had a decision to make, and I didn't have a lot of time to make it. In some ways my whole professional life has been like that: You have this great opportunity; it's going to turn your life upside down; we need an answer by morning. Go.

I chose the job. I went back to Channel 11. It was a huge risk. The industry was in flux. Nothing was guaranteed. But I'd made my call: this unreliable, unstable media world would be mine.

I still occasionally hear from the odd student from that apprentice teaching year. They reach out. One of them, Evron Joseph, became an IT specialist and went on to work at Black-Berry. He invited me to his wedding and keeps in touch via social media. I am so touched by that.

And I remember how it felt to see the light in a student's eyes when they were learning.

The truth is, I am a natural teacher. Even when daunted by all those young faces looking up from their desks, I felt comfortable and confident at the front of the classroom. I felt I was making an impact. But journalism, I loved. I had a heart for it. It didn't come easy. It was challenging. It put a bit of fear in me—and I liked that.

People have said to me that as a journalist, I'm still teaching. I'm telling people stories, enlightening them. I think they're right. In a way, making the choice I did, I got to do both.

This is politics: don't be afraid

As CHCH-TV's official Queen's Park reporter, it was my job to provide the station with breaking news reports on the provincial government. Policy changes. Budgets. Controversies.

I was young, still in my twenties. It was a great opportunity. The only problem was, frankly, I was scared of political reporting. I didn't think it was my strong suit. I was a solid feature reporter. I was good at doing longer stories, at writing. Politics wasn't my thing.

Which is one of the reasons I wanted to prove to myself that I could do it.

So, there's a provincial budget coming down the pipe. It's my job to report on its key elements, make sure Channel 11 viewers get the information they need and want. Do I list all the different aspects of the budget—here's what's going to be cut, here's where the government will increase spending?

If you just start quoting the numbers, your viewers' eyes will glaze over. It's too much.

Instead, I spoke to a family and related how the budget would work for them. Here's the Smith family they have a boy and a girl. The girl plays hockey. Because of this particular change in the budget, this family now gets a tax break because the daughter plays hockey.

That's how my reporting evolved. OK, fine, premier, you said this. But how does that affect the real people who are out there in your community? You said this about homelessness, so I'll go and see if I can find a homeless person to give us their perspective. There were so many ways that I could relate things to real people, and in that respect, my reporting became a whole lot better. When people understand a change in government policy means "I'm going to be paying this much more for gas" or "My family and I will have to do a staycation instead of a vacation because our dollar won't be what it was in the US"—whatever it was, I found real people to bring that policy change to life, and that transformed it from something vague into something viewers could care about and understand. And something I could care about, too. For my reporting to connect with viewers, that was key: I had to care. For it to strike a chord with them, it had to also matter to me.

It might have been tempting, when the post at Queen's Park came up, to tell my boss at Channel 11 I didn't really see myself as a political reporter. That I wanted to do more in-depth news, more feature work, and less daily political coverage. Part of me wanted to say, *Politics? That's just not me.* But Queen's Park, provincial politics, was the opportunity that came my way, so I took it. Not only did I prove to myself I could do a job that I found intimidating, I became a better journalist. Because to cover politics, to cover it in a way that excited me, I had to push myself. I had to think outside the box.

Nobody said this life stuff, this career stuff, would be easy. I never *expected* it to be easy, and that makes all the difference.

Draft pick

When I worked as the Queen's Park reporter for CHCH-TV in the mid-nineties, most of the journalists covering the provincial legislature were men. But I wasn't the only woman in the press gallery. A few of us formed an alliance, a kind of brat pack: along with me there was Monica Kim, who was with Global Television back then, and Allison Vuchnich of CFTO, CTV's local station for Toronto. Amid the bastion of white men, we were all young women, in our twenties, covering provincial politics: one Korean woman, one Black woman, and a white woman with a last name that people kept wanting her to change.

Can't you just shorten that up a bit?

Um, no. That's my name, thanks.

We helped each other. More than that, we looked out for each other. We relied on each other. We became friends.

At Queen's Park, there was generally a story of the day: one big story that would be told by different news crews in different ways. If the premier was speaking and Monica couldn't be there at one o'clock because she was interviewing someone in their home, say, about how the budget would affect families, I might share my clips from the press conference with her. Because you just can't *be* two places at once. If Allison had a great position at the front of a scrum, I'd hand her my mic and she'd hold it up with hers. We would help each other out like that.

Had they known, I don't think our bosses would have approved. We were, strictly speaking, competitors. But we didn't believe we had to function that way, or even that to do so would best serve our work and our stations' viewers. In reality, every reporter, every station, is going to run some version of the story of the day, and their regular viewers are going to watch it. Rather than trying to beat each other to the best quote or shot, we helped each other ensure all of our reports were full and complete. And through supporting each other that way, we eliminated some of the strife from the extremely high-pressure environment of daily news.

How far can such alliances go in the dog-eat-dog world of television journalism?

I'll tell you how far.

In 1997, while we three women were reporting on Queen's Park for our respective stations, CTV embarked on plans to launch CTV News One (now CTV News Channel), its answer to CNN Headline News. They were building a new team to feed this twenty-four-hour beast. It was a massive hiring. It was at this time that Lisa LaFlamme, Dawna Friesen and many other now-veteran journalists were hired by CTV. The network reached out to Monica Kim, asking her to come in for an interview. She went in for an audition and gave them some tapes of her work to review.

Now here's the kind of friend she was. Monica comes back from CTV and says, "You know what, Marci? They haven't seen you, maybe, because you're working for Channel 11." (A regional station, so it wasn't exactly prominent outside of Hamilton.) "They may not know your work, but I think you'd be perfect for this." She gave me the name of the administrative assistant for the head of news, Henry Kowalski. "Give them a call," she said, "and see if they'll see you."

I took Monica's advice. I called. I thought even if they could look at the tape and give me some constructive criticism, it would be worthwhile.

They called me in, and I had an interview with Henry. I told him about myself and my work so far but also, because he was interested, about my background: how my parents had come to this country from Trinidad, and it was just us here. When my grandparents left Trinidad, they went to New York, so I have only immediate family in Canada; everyone else is in Brooklyn. It was a great discussion. I asked him if he could check my tape and give me feedback, tell me if I need improvement. He thanked me for coming. And that was that.

At least, I thought it was.

That was early summer 1997. A little later, sometime in August, I was at a conference in Chicago organized by the

National Association of Black Journalists. I'd taken a bus down from Toronto with a bunch of fellow Black reporters, including Dwight. We'd remained close as we both steadily progressed in our careers. When we went down for the Chicago conference, Dwight was a crime reporter with City TV News. We were keen. The keynote speaker that year was Bill Clinton. It was a big deal.

So there we were in Chicago, geared up for a jam-packed weekend, ready to hobnob with colleagues from all over the States, to get right down to the nitty-gritty with our fellow journalists of colour about the challenges we faced and also the opportunities we had, in our roles, to make a difference.

Then this call came through to my hotel room. I picked it up, and the man on the other end said, "Marci, this is Robert Hearst from CTV News. We've been looking for you."

I kept my voice steady. This was CTV's vice-president of news, calling me in a hotel room in Chicago. This man had gone to the trouble of tracking me down. I said, "Hi, Mr. Hearst. How did you find me?"

He explained that they had tried looking me up, but my number was unlisted. They'd tried to find my family, even looked for my relatives in Brooklyn. Finally, they'd ended up calling the desk at Channel 11. As a reporter, you always leave contact information at work for where you'll be in case a major news event takes place and you need to be called back into the station in a hurry. Calling the station would probably have been CTV's last resort, though, because there was no guarantee that someone at my current job would readily tell a bigwig from another television station how to find me. But it happened that working on the desk that day was a friend of mine, Deborah Walker. She said, "I think she'll want to hear from you," and gave him the name and number of my hotel.

He was calling to offer me a job. Except there was a catch. The job wasn't in Toronto, as I'd instantly, foolishly, thought it would be. It was in Halifax.

"You're our last hire," he said. "You would be a reporter and producer on our news team covering the Atlantic provinces. I need a decision by tomorrow morning."

I had to collect myself. I definitely didn't see this coming. I had twenty-four hours to decide, and the job would start in a couple of weeks. That meant picking up and moving to a new city, on the east coast, hundreds of kilometres from home, with barely any time to think about what that meant, or even whether it was something I wanted to do.

During my years with Channel 11, I'd travelled all over the country. Not for work, but with my mom. Mom had long since finished her accounting studies and become a provincial tax auditor. She'd be sent somewhere, Vancouver, say, to conduct an audit on an organization and set up there for a week. I would align my vacation time with these trips, and travel with her or meet her there. During the days, I'd explore the city, visit museums and find the best places to eat so Mom and I could go out together for a nice dinner. Mom would finish work on the Friday and we'd stay in town for the weekend to spend some time together. Through those trips, I got to know my mom better than I had growing up. I also got to know this huge country we live in.

Halifax, however, happened to be one place Mom had never been sent for an audit. I'd never set foot there. It wasn't just that I didn't know the city at all. In my mind, this was a big leap, from little CHCH-TV in Hamilton to the national news. I was scared.

I called home. I talked it over with my sister. My parents. Lloyd—we weren't married yet, but he was my boyfriend. Everybody said I had to do this. It was a great opportunity.

Then I called Dwight, who had a room in the same hotel, and asked him to come over. I needed his advice. We had a long conversation. Finally he said, "Marci, you have to take it. It's the national news. You *can't* say no."

He was right. I didn't say no. I accepted the job. I came back home on the Sunday. I remember my dad taking me to Queen's Park. One of the lovely security guards opened my office for me. I cleaned it out. On the Monday morning, we drove to Hamilton. I was partway through my two weeks' vacation, so I wouldn't be going back to work. They accepted my notice and wished me the best.

I began preparations to relocate my life and to tackle a new phase in my career.

First, though, I called Henry. I thanked him. I knew he was taking a chance on me. Henry put it this way: "It's not all about what you are now—it's what I believe you'll become. You're my draft pick, Marci."

A long list of people believed in me enough to help me make that leap to the national news. Monica, my family, Dwight. And my new boss, Henry.

All these years later, I'm still grateful for what they all saw in me, when I wasn't sure I saw it myself. This is what I mean when I tell people, especially younger folks just starting to find their way in a career, to find their "tribe": that select group of people they can trust to know them well, to be frank and honest, and to support them when support is required, whether it be advice, an ear or a pep talk. Your tribe might be really small; it might be one or two friends, a sibling, a parent. It might not even contain any colleagues. But it must be steadfast, clear-eyed and true—true, especially, to you.

Home is where your friends are

After resigning from CHCH-TV, I attended a CTV session about what to expect, and what was expected of us, as new journalists in the CTV fold. But there's no training or info session for how to pick up your life, move three provinces away and start a new job—one that will test you, challenge you, push your limits—in the space of under two weeks.

My first home in Halifax was a hotel. That's where I lived while getting accustomed to the bureau and looking for a place to call my own. In a situation like that, you need to call on your supports. Luckily, Aretha and Sherri Borden, who were sisters and also Haligonians, had flown to Toronto earlier in the summer and had ridden the bus with us to Chicago for the Black journalism convention. Aretha was a teacher and Sherri a print journalist. We had gotten to know each other and gotten along well. They had grown up in New Glasgow, a couple of hours away from Halifax, on the coast. Their dad, Sparky Paris, was a boxing legend who had been inducted into the Canadian Boxing Hall of Fame.

Sherri and Aretha were two of the first people I told after I accepted the job offer from CTV: "Hey, guess what? I'm moving to your city!" They urged me to call them when I got to town: We'll show you around, help you get settled.

I called, and they did. They took great care of me and gave me a rundown on the community. They offered insight on a different side of Halifax than the one most Canadians see, one filled with racial disparity and illustrated by the destruction of Africville, a close-knit Black community that, when it existed, had its own stores, a post office, a school and a church. The city of Halifax had refused to provide amenities for Africville that other Haligonians took for granted. There was no garbage disposal, access to clean water (the people there relied on wells) or sewage. Instead of providing these services to ensure a safe and healthy environment for the residents, the city actually put a waste disposal site in the area in the late 1950s. A decade later, Africville was condemned and its residents forcibly relocated by the city, which bulldozed their homes and community buildings, including Seaview Baptist Church. It's a dark part of Canadian history that doesn't get the attention it deserves.

Aretha took me to North Preston and Cherry Brook, outside Dartmouth, both predominantly Black communities. In Cherry Brook, we visited the Black Cultural Centre for Nova

Scotia. She also introduced me to her church in downtown Halifax, with its amazing choir.

One Sunday, a young woman from New Brunswick came to the church with her family. She performed, and the pastor said they'd be taking an offering: they were raising funds for this girl to go to Toronto where she would further study opera. She was incredible: a true prodigy. We ended up doing a national piece on her, as part of this series we called *Success Stories*, which was like a "hometown heroes" feature. The piece was put together in Toronto with clips from me. The girl was Measha Brueggergosman, who's now a major figure in the music world and a national treasure. Years later, our paths crossed again, and we've become great friends.

My friendship with Aretha and Sherri really deepened my understanding of the community and my connection to it, which broadened the scope of my reporting. But more than that, it helped Halifax feel like home.

Going national

I t was a right-to-die story. My first piece for the national news.
A huge thing.

Twenty-one years before Canada's medical assistance
in dying legislation came into effect in 2018, an incident in
Halifax made national news. As per his family's wishes, a crit-
ically ill cancer patient named Paul Mills had been taken off
life support and had been expected to die shortly afterward.
Instead, his suffering and distress had only increased, even
after receiving abnormally high doses of palliative narcotics.
Several months later, Halifax police raided the Queen Elizabeth II Health Sciences Centre and charged respirologist
Nancy Morrison with first-degree murder for administering an
injection of potassium-chloride—a compound that can stop
the heart—to Mills directly before his death.

The case sparked national interest because it touched a nerve. There was a large grey area in the medical system. Where was the line between a doctor performing active euthanasia (or what was then known as assisted suicide—doing something to deliberately hasten a patient's death) and easing the discomfort of a dying person by giving them high doses of such drugs as morphine, a common practice that can, as a side effect, cause patients to die more quickly than they otherwise might?

In midsummer, a couple of months after Dr. Morrison had been charged, I began my job with CTV National News in Halifax. Morrison was still making headlines. Her story, and its relation to all those difficult questions about end-of-life care and our legal system, became my first.

In my report, I broke down the Criminal Code. We had first-degree murder. Second-degree murder. There was nothing for euthanasia. What do you do when this person is dying and, because there is no hope, wants to speed up their death? This important question was of significance to the whole country, our medical system and our laws.

This story was a far cry from the local fire I'd reported on as a rookie at Channel 11 all those years before. It was bigger potatoes than the fiscal and political woes of the Ontario government, which had lately been my beat. Who knew that by going way out east to Halifax I'd drop right into the midst of something so urgent and so controversial? It was powerful stuff.

The anchor that night was Lloyd Robertson. Before my report he said, "Tonight, we welcome the newest member of our Atlantic bureau, Marci Ien." I felt pride. I felt nervous: I was going on-air. Nationwide.

That story has stayed with me, and thinking back to it, considering where we are now on end-of-life issues, I realize the Nancy Morrison case definitely contributed to change—to the conversations and the on-the-ground work that finally led to change. I didn't know then that it would. But I knew it was a story that mattered and that it was my job to tell it.

Afterward I received an email from Craig Oliver, who was CTV's Ottawa bureau chief. It read, "Welcome to the family, kid."

I emailed back a thank you, but I really wanted to say so much more to him that night. I will never forget his kindness in taking the time to acknowledge my work. To welcome me. It might have been a small gesture to him, but it meant the world to me.

Heavy Black population

I made another good friend the year I moved to Halifax. Erin, who was married to Shawn, one of our camera operators, was also a journalist, working for the local station. Originally from Vancouver, Erin had attended the University of Ottawa, where she met Shawn when he was working for CTV's Ottawa bureau. Then Shawn was posted to Halifax, and eastward they came.

Both new to the city, Erin and I discovered it together. I felt like I had an ally. She was my person. We tried out new restaurants and spent Saturdays driving out of the city to places like Wolfville or Lunenburg, checking out little museums and the shops in beautiful Mahone Bay.

There's a story Erin liked to tell, and that I still like to share, about when she and Shawn first arrived in Halifax. Like me, they were staying in a hotel while they house hunted. Erin is blond-haired and blue-eyed. Shawn is also white. They were eating in the hotel restaurant one day and talking over their plans about looking for a place to live. Overhearing their conversation, a server decided to offer some advice: "Stay away from the North End," she said. "Heavy Black population." Erin didn't skip a beat: "I don't mind overweight people. Black, white or otherwise."

Despite their server's "warning," or perhaps in defiance of it, Erin and Shawn did move to the North End, a part of town that did indeed boast a "heavy" Black population: many of the people who lived there had been displaced from Africville.

Meanwhile, I chose a place in the South End near Dalhousie University. I remember my friend Aretha, who had been the one to introduce me to the history of the local Black community, saying, "Marci, our mothers are maids there."

At first, this observation gave me pause. Why was I moving to what was, in the local sense, the very opposite of the Black community?

But the truth is, I like how Erin, Shawn and I flipped expectations of where we would settle down. They in the north, me in the south: that's how integration works. It harkens back to the corporate world as well and why diversity is so important in the workplace: people bringing different ideas and experiences to the table. Understanding and empathy both begin when we cross those false boundaries.

No stupid questions

I'd done it: I'd made the leap from local news on a regional station in Hamilton to a national network. I was getting a handle on my new duties, growing into my role.

Then, three months in, boom—I was recalled to Toronto. The network needed me to fill in for a maternity leave. My move was the result of a domino effect. The mat leave was for a person on staff at the investigative show *W5*. Someone from *Canada AM* was reassigned to fill her role, while Lisa LaFlamme, the weekend anchor on CTV News Channel— who also reported for CTV National News three days a week— was shifting to *Canada AM*. I would take over Lisa's duties.

I moved back to Ontario, leaving my car with Erin and Shawn, and I promised my landlord that I would continue to pay rent while away. I didn't want to give up my apartment.

When I showed up for my weekend of training under Lisa, she asked me if I'd ever anchored before. The anchor is the main person presenting the news on a TV news program, the role in which so many Canadians would have seen CTV's Lloyd Robertson and CBC's Peter Mansbridge over the decades. It's the person behind the desk who reads the headlines, introduces reports from journalists in the field, and conducts interviews with experts and pundits on breaking news. (Nowadays, there might not be a desk, the anchor might be standing, and the role might even be shared among a few veteran journalists.)

Obviously, I had no anchor experience, and that's what I told her: "No. None."

"OK," she said. "You've told me. No need to tell anyone else. Do not repeat that." That's Lisa. She doesn't mince words. And she gives great advice.

I watched as she read her newscasts and conducted her interviews, then I got in the chair and attempted to do the same. I had so much to learn. Anchoring was nothing like going into the field, gathering footage, conducting interviews and piecing together your report. It meant being able to fly by the seat of your pants. This was a twenty-four-hour news service. You were reporting on news as it broke, and you might not have much information. You're on the air and guests are thrown at you. I watched Lisa and noted her poise when she was conducting an interview. There weren't many facts to go on. She used open-ended questions. She'd say, "Tell me more about that." Nothing where a guest could easily answer yes or no. I learned the importance of putting yourself in the viewer's seat: What would they want to know? I took on the creed that there are no stupid questions. And I reminded myself that even when things were changing by the minute, we were telling viewers a story. It was my job to lay the story out. There's going to be a start, there's got to be a middle, there has to be a finish. Just lay it out.

As the weeks passed, my comfort level grew. I got better. I felt stronger. I returned to Halifax eight months later with some serious new experience under my belt. And I was going to need it, as the biggest story of my young career would soon break.

"Tell me about your brother"

It was late evening on September 2, 1998, a little over a year after I'd begun reporting nationally from Atlantic Canada. I was in my Halifax apartment reading, about to get ready for bed. The phone rang. The national news assignment desk was on the line from Toronto. There was word that a plane had crashed off the coast. Details were scarce. They didn't know the size of the plane, where it was from or the number of people on it—but they wanted me to be ready to go into work. I hung up.

Minutes later, the phone rang again. *Get into the bureau. It's a jetliner. More than two hundred people on board.* I got dressed and rushed out the door.

The station was abuzz. Every reporter, editor, writer—everybody who worked at the station—was in. And I mean everybody.

People were bustling about, doing jobs they would not normally do. People were being asked: Can you check this? Can you check that? Some were on the line to emergency services; others were getting equipment up and ready. Could they get a signal?

What was happening? What had caused this crash? Could there be any survivors? We just didn't know.

As details emerged, we learned that Swissair Flight 111 had been less than an hour into its overnight trip from New York's JFK Airport to Geneva, Switzerland, when it fell out of the sky into the ocean near Peggy's Cove, a small coastal community and famous tourist site renowned for its iconic lighthouse. Calls went out from the newsroom to anyone in Peggy's Cove any of us knew—local fishers, anyone—to find out what they'd seen or heard.

I was among those dispatched directly to Peggy's Cove. We hit the road and drove the forty-five kilometres southwest from Halifax, down an increasingly winding rural highway. It was late evening, pitch-black, by the time we arrived. This wasn't like an urban area lit up with street lights. We couldn't see much at all.

People were out, though, emergency crews down by the shore, as well as locals. We walked around, looked for people to talk to and asked them what they knew. When we reported on the situation for *Canada* AM the next morning, the story we told was, in part, about the immediate rescue response from the close-knit community. Private boats from around St. Margaret's Bay were among the first to arrive at the crash site. Our cameras had captured this, as well as footage of floating debris. Some local people were traumatized that night because they had gone out hoping to rescue survivors but instead were seeing body parts in the water or bringing them up in nets. It became clear very quickly that there would be no rescue. This was a recovery operation.

That first night and the following day, we worked for at least eighteen hours straight.

It had been an international flight and the passenger roster reflected that: 136 passengers from the United States, thirty from France, twenty-eight from Switzerland, six from Britain, three from Italy, three from Germany, two from Greece, and solitary passengers from Iran, Spain, Yugoslavia, Afghanistan, St. Kitts and Nevis, Russia, and Saudi Arabia. As the week progressed, and as we drove back and forth from Halifax reporting on new developments—findings from the Transportation Safety Board, the discovery of the black box, the investigation on the water and the investigation above ground—family members began arriving from all over the world. They came by the busload to this small fishing village, the shattered relatives of passengers and crew, looking for answers. They'd walk to the shore, look out to sea, try to make sense of the tragedy. They would embrace, huddled together. Some would toss bouquets of flowers into the water. Then they would head back to their bus and another group of family members would get off the next bus and have their time to grieve at the site where their loved ones had been lost.

It was so devastating. It really, really hurt. What do you say to these people who have lost so much? How do you throw a microphone in their faces? This was my first experience reporting on a tragedy of this magnitude, and the fact is, I didn't feel altogether comfortable doing my job. I wrestled with it. We tried to be respectful. If people didn't want to talk, they didn't. When they did, they did. And then I tried to ask questions: *What do you remember? Tell me about your brother. Tell me about your husband. Tell me about your wife.* I knew that when a person turned into a news story, they became a number, one of the many people who died. Victims are reduced to photographs. Hundreds and hundreds of pictures not representing the lives lived at all. So that became my focus. There were 229 victims, and we didn't know anything about them—the kind of people they were, the contributions they'd made to the world . . . only that they'd become part of this huge story. So I tried to break it down to the actual people and the individual lives that had been lost.

When I wasn't in Peggy's Cove, I was in an editing suite in our news bureau in Halifax, poring over tape, looking for clips and visuals to be used in that evening's news story. In part, when reviewing footage like that, you are looking through things to make sure they are acceptable for the general audience. In the process you see horrific things, the stuff of nightmares, images that you can't later *unsee*. I will never forget watching the video of one woman who, when approaching the water, handed her baby to a volunteer and tried to throw herself into the sea. Volunteers stopped her and she was taken into care.

There was also a massive international media presence: NBC, CBS, ABC. The world came to Peggy's Cove to report on every step of the investigation. It was a lot for such a small community to endure on top of the tragedy itself. I remember a priest from one of the local churches. He seemed to always be there, offering support to the families and local residents. The church was kept open all hours so people could come for quiet, to pray, to reflect. I wondered how he maintained his strength. So one day, I asked him. "You are a source of support for so many right now. Who do *you* turn to when you're feeling low?"

"I look up," he said. "God has put me in this place at this time."

I never forgot his words.

After weeks of covering the crash, after the adrenalin that had kept me going began to subside, I found myself emotionally and physically exhausted. But I also felt guilty. Who was I to complain about the toll of this crash on me when people had lost their loved ones? A senior producer encouraged me to take some time off, and I did. I took a few days. I find as reporters, we see a lot, we witness and process terrible things, and the effect that can have often just isn't mentioned. I needed some time to take a breath, to feel restored, and I was happy I took it.

Looking back, all these years later, what stands out are the acts of kindness. There were so many kindnesses that pierced through the darkness of that tragedy. The fishers who had jumped in their boats the night of the crash. The locals who offered comfort to families through meals and hot tea. The Coast Guard captain who left a note on a stuffed *Lion King* toy that had been retrieved from the crash site. It read, "It was carefully washed with the hope that it might provide some family member with solace as a tangible connection with the child to whom it belonged." As the late children's television host Fred Rogers used to famously say, "When I was a boy and I would see scary things in the news, my mother would say to me, 'Look for the helpers.' You will always find people who are helping."

Peggy's Cove, Nova Scotia, had an abundant supply.

Home is where your sister is

In 1999, I returned to Ontario. It was time to be back in the family fold. I also wanted to push myself career-wise. I needed to grow more professionally—to be challenged. And to be in the game meant being in Toronto. The network allowed me to transfer in exchange for temporarily giving up my full-time status. I came back to anchor CTV News Channel two days a week and report as a freelancer for CTV News. Some weeks I was called in every day; some weeks, just once or twice.

My sister, Lorraine, was a busy realtor and had recently divorced. She had three daughters: two-year-old Sari, nine-year-old Jordy and sixteen-year-old Mellie. She also had a downstairs bedroom I could move into. I'd always been close with my nieces and moving in felt like coming home.

What a privilege it was just to be part of their lives. And I was so glad that I could help: with expenses and with the kids. Because I was on weekend shifts as a news anchor and free on the weekdays I hadn't been called into work, I could do things like drive Mellie to her arts-focused high school, which was in another district and a long trip on public transit. Jordy played basketball and ran track, and I was able to go watch many of her meets and games. I spent time with Sari, who was still so young, and gave my sister a break.

Lorraine often worked evenings showing houses or had early-morning meetings with clients and then afternoons off, while I often had whole days off. With our respective interesting careers and their unpredictable schedules, we sometimes found ourselves home with a few spare hours in the middle of the day. That's when we'd curl up on her basement couch and indulge in movies from the 1950s and '60s. Can you say Doris Day, Cary Grant, Rock Hudson, Sophia Loren? We watched *Pillow Talk*, *Charade* and the romantic comedy *Houseboat*. And we ate way too much. Much of which involved chocolate. We still joke about whether any of our clothes fit us at the time. We were happy. We had each other.

This was before I had a family of my own. I've always said my sister's daughters were my first set of kids. I'll tell people I have five kids, not just two. I lived with my sister for a couple of years before I got married, watching her in action, knee-deep with her in the fray of a busy household and family life. I'm not sure I fully knew it at the time, but I was learning how it was done: mothering, managing home life and career, holding it all together.

Lorraine is practical—a problem solver and a doer. She's

professional, stylish, efficient: not only will she sell your house, but she'll stage it first so it's ready for sale with minimal fuss and enviable results. Those aren't my skills, but I can relate to what Lorraine brings to her work that makes her so effective: She asks questions, and she listens well. She learns what people are looking for, what they most want. She's tuned in to her clients the way a good journalist is tuned in to an interview subject.

She was also tuned in to her kids. They all grew up with passions. Jordy, the middle daughter, after earning a business degree, is now an elite runner with the Olympics in her sights. Mellie, her eldest, competed as a debater in law school and is now a writer who focuses on race, inclusion and equity. Sari, her youngest—brilliantly gifted—was top of her class at university and has been accepted into law school. Lorraine scheduled her appointments around their commitments. Somehow she made it all work. And later, when her ex-husband, who's now deceased, had brain cancer, she helped take care of him.

Because that's Lorraine. This is the woman who, amid all the demands and family responsibilities, her work and her recently failed marriage, remembered her kid sister. Took me in, set me up in a bedroom, kept me close. Here's what I can tell you for sure: that kind of care is contagious.

Lorraine—who asked for a sister, for *me*, way back at the age of seven; who taught me how to love completely; who poured into me the power of empathy. When someone showers you with love like that, you can't help but love that way yourself. She's my ground zero for love—my base. She's the reason I love hard. That kind of love, though, isn't always reciprocated.

Maybe that kind of full love can be taught and caught only by those who have a capacity for it. Who are open to it. Who are vulnerable. Being vulnerable takes courage. That kind of love is risky. It's also hard to find.

The kids! (*From left*: my niece Sari; my daughter, Blaize; my son, Dash; my nieces Jordanne and Melayna.)

Season's tickets

My dad had offered to buy my wedding dress. I had exactly what I wanted in mind, but it's hard to describe the dress you imagine. I tried to help a friend, a fellow news anchor, picture it: something floaty, not traditional, not white, more of a beige or neutral colour. She was walking down Queen Street East in downtown Toronto, saw a dress in a shop window, and thought, *That's Marci's dress.*

My dad and I drove down together to this little indie shop. It was the same day basketball star Vince Carter was deciding whether to extend his contract with the Toronto Raptors. The Raptors were still an upstart team, and Vince had been the best thing that happened to them yet. Nerves were high that day among fans—my dad and me included. What would become of the team if Vince left?

We paused before getting out of the car and turned up the radio. We had it tuned to 680 News, where we knew the live press conference would be broadcast. We heard Vince announce what we'd most wanted but hardly dared hope: he was going to stay. My dad and I screamed with joy and hugged. We were so happy. We'd always gone to sporting events together over the years, the odd baseball or football game. But once the Raptors had come to town, that had been our sport, and we'd gone to many games. We both loved basketball's clip, the speed of the game. It's non-stop, an exciting two and a half hours. You never found yourself partway through a basketball game, as we had more than once while watching the Toronto Blue Jays, wondering how much longer before it was over, or why a particular pitcher—Juan Guzman, say, who was famous for this—had to take his sweet time between every pitch.

It was more than the pace of basketball, though, that drew us and kept us. It's a ball—that's it. You have to navigate your way around the court, you have to practise, but anybody from anywhere can pick up a basketball and learn to play. It doesn't cost much. It's an equalizer—an equal-opportunity sport.

The players' individual stories bear this out. I love the stories of athletes' lives, the dramas in the ESPN *30 for 30* documentaries—but it's the basketball players' stories that I love most. Take retired Philadelphia 76er Allen Iverson. He came from a single-parent household and had a sister with disabilities. Basketball was a way out: for his sister and for him. So many of the players have humble backgrounds or actual tragedies in their early lives: lost parents, health challenges in their families. These guys have something to prove—and they prove it on the court.

In the car outside the dress shop, in the midst of our excitement, I said to Dad, "Maybe we get season's tickets. That way, so what if I'm married—we still have a date at least once a week."

And that's what we did. We bought season's tickets. I got married. I had a daughter. Seven years later, I had a son. I moved through several stages in my career. My marriage broke down. I started over. Through it all, every week for nearly twenty years, sometimes twice a week, my dad and I would park our cars at York Mills station, hop on the subway and go to a Raptors game together. That was our catch-up time. We'd talk about our weeks, the stories I'd covered at work, the family.

As fans, we watched the Raptors grow from an upstart franchise to a championship team, from a stadium they could scarcely fill to nightly sellouts. We delighted in watching Rookie-of-the-Year Damon Stoudamire's moves on the court. Likewise my all-time favourite player, the gritty point guard Alvin Williams. We watched Vince Carter become "Air Canada" with his massive dunks (who will ever forget the NBC All-Star Slam Dunk Contest in 2000?). We followed DeMar DeRozan's meteoric rise and the trade that sent him south. I would say on the air and off that the Raptors were Canada's team—the only team in the NBA and the only professional sports team with a roster diverse enough that any Canadian kid could see themself on that bench, that court—imagine rising to that level. Heroes should come in all shapes, sizes and colours: a living reminder that it's possible, with perseverance and a huge dose of grit, to get where you want to go.

That's the message I want my kids and my sister's kids—the next generation in our family—to take in, be it consciously or subconsciously. My dad has slowed down; he doesn't get to every game these days. It saddens me. But we'll keep those seats for our family. In its way, this tradition Dad and I started has become a legacy.

Hanging out with my dad at a Toronto Raptors game.

Wedding photo

In the photo from my wedding, Mellie is crying and I'm hugging her.

They aren't tears of joy. My sister's eldest daughter was happy for me that day, don't get me wrong. But I know what she was thinking: This marriage meant more than me and Lloyd embarking on a future together. It meant a time in our lives together, Mellie's and mine, was coming to a close.

I have mentioned that when I returned to Toronto from Halifax, I moved in with my sister and her kids. Well, I lived there for two years. I didn't leave until Lloyd and I got married in the fall of 2001. The date was set for September 25, and the plan was to travel, with close friends and family in tow, to St. Thomas, in the US Virgin Islands. We would partake of an

Eastern Caribbean cruise, disembark and exchange our vows in warm sunshine on an island paradise.

Exactly fourteen days prior to the big day, however, 9/11 happened. As a result of the devastation, death and rampant fear, airports all over North American were shuttered. Aside from processing that catastrophic event and what it might mean for the world as we knew it, we had our own private challenge to navigate. We had this destination wedding planned, and we had to decide what to do, and fast. Cancel? Postpone? Enact a quick reboot and shift the proceedings closer to home?

We knew that some key wedding guests would have to travel regardless: Lloyd's best man, for one, lived in New York City. We decided it was too late to change course. We let everyone know: we're doing this, we're moving forward. If you can't make it, we understand. We were delighted to find all our guests willing to make the trip.

There was all that agonizing, that shadow—the bitter aftermath of a disastrous terror attack—but also the joy of a ceremony among close family and friends. The breathtaking beach, the healing waters, the hot sun. The two of us embarking on a new phase in our lives together.

And Mellie. When I look back to that day, it's this photograph of Mellie and me that, often as not, comes to mind. I was thirteen when Mellie (short for Melayna) was born. In the photograph, I am thirty-two and she is nineteen, a young woman. It was taken right after the ceremony, which took place poolside. Mellie was standing close by and looked emotional—as if she might start crying. I immediately went to hug her and held her tight. We take up the whole picture.

In some senses, we'd grown up together. Those two years of living together under the same roof were rich with good moments and memories—with a sisterly closeness that wasn't going to stay quite the same. Before taking Mellie in my arms that day—in front of a camera I didn't know was going to cap-ture us—I caught the truth of this in her eyes. I knew what she was thinking: *I'm going to miss you. I'm going to miss us.*

I squeezed her, hard. Because so was I.

Election baby

June 28, 2004: I stood on the Danforth outside then-NDP-leader Jack Layton's headquarters, microphone in hand, filing my last report for *Canada AM* before going on maternity leave. It was federal election day, and I was very pregnant. I'd been lucky with the pregnancy: there was no discomfort, no strife. I felt healthy and strong. Optimistic. It had always been my plan to work right up until election day, and I'd made it. Paul Martin would win a minority that day, keeping the Liberals in power for just a bit longer before the next election, when Stephen Harper's Conservatives would nudge them out.

I put my microphone away, my mind already turning to the coming weeks, when I would finally have the chance to prepare for this new person about to emerge into our lives. Because election time is so busy on a news program, I'd done very little on the baby front—we didn't even have a crib. Now was the time to shop, to organize and to see some friends. One day, I had a lunch date with a friend, a fellow news anchor. I went to a doctor's appointment that morning, planning to head to lunch afterward. But while at the appointment, my water broke. My doctor said, "I'm phoning the hospital to let them know you're coming. I know you—you'll go home and putter around. I'm calling to tell them to expect you. You have to go home, grab your bag and get to the hospital."

So I never met my friend. I had to phone the restaurant and let them know I wouldn't make it. I drove home and told Lloyd, who was working from the house that day, we have to get to the hospital, like, now.

Our daughter Blaize was born on July 10. I thought I'd have more time to get ready for her, but she came early. You know what, though? As soon as she was here, I realized I was ready, more than ready, to share my life with her. It was summertime, lovely to go outside. She came everywhere with me. We did everything together. If my niece had a basketball game, I'd pack Blaize in the car and we'd go. We'd drive into midtown Toronto for story time at Mabel's Fables bookstore. It was such a neat, supportive environment; I loved going there. We'd go to the Movies for Mommies film showings at the Cineplex at Fairview Mall. When Blaize wasn't yet six months old, my boss at *Canada AM* had a St. Lucia Day celebration. She's Swedish and makes these amazing meatballs for her annual party. I brought Blaize and put her down in her car seat in the middle of the party for a couple of hours. We lived life like that, together.

I didn't take a full year off with her, just nine or ten months. I'd told work that I wouldn't take leave for a whole year; I think I felt like they'd need me. But once I was home with Blaize, as the months passed, I wondered why I'd said that. They had me covered, of course. And I wanted more time. It was hard to go back to work at that point. But I had committed to it, and so I gritted my teeth, sorted out childcare and went.

Back to the camera, back to the fast pace of daily news. It was the same as it had always been, yet it wasn't the same at all. I had a whole new world to come home to after each shift.

Sierra Leone

I was wrapping up after a *Canada AM* shift and had gone back to my desk to reply to some emails before heading home. My phone rang, and on the other end of the line was Ben Peterson. Ben had co-founded Journalists for Human Rights with Alexandra Sicotte-Levesque. Ben explained that JHR's mission was to "empower journalists to cover human rights stories objectively and effectively." JHR had partnered with hundreds of organizations in two dozen countries to train thousands of journalists whose stories reached more than sixty million people. JHR now wanted to partner with me.

Ben asked if I'd be willing to travel to Sierra Leone to evaluate JHR's operations there. Sierra Leone had been decimated by an eleven-year civil war. More than fifty thousand people had been killed. Hundreds of thousands displaced. The Revolutionary

United Front had attempted, with support from the special forces of Charles Taylor's National Patriotic Front of Liberia, to overthrow the government and had plunged the country into bloody conflict. It was against this backdrop—of a country trying to rise again from the ashes of war, to rebuild, while putting to trial in the Special Court for Sierra Leone those responsible for the attempted coup and mass bloodshed—that the JHR set up shop.

The program had been running for a little more than a year with a handful of Canadian journalists mentoring and working with their Sierra Leonean counterparts.

Ben thought ten to fourteen days would give me enough time to assess the situation: whether the program was meeting its goals, what was working, what wasn't, and to meet with reporters at various media houses. Trouble was, the trip was planned for September, which is like New Year's in the television world. It's premiere month. A new slate of shows, a brand-new season of *Canada AM*. I went to my executive producer's office the next day—armed with info—to ask for the time off. She saw my excitement and met me in the middle. She granted me seven days off but only if I left on a Friday and included a weekend, which made the trip ten days total. We could work with that.

I said goodbye to Lloyd and Blaize (she was four years old) on a Friday evening in September 2008 and boarded a plane for Heathrow in London. Once there, I had hours to spare before my connecting flight. I grabbed a bite to eat and passed the time reading the notes for my upcoming assignment. When my flight was finally called, I boarded, relieved I was one step closer to my final destination. When I landed in Lungi, it took

a while to retrieve my luggage and even longer for security officers to check it. I was exhausted. It was hot, and I had one
more mode of transportation to take: a ferry. The airport and
the capital city—Freetown—are separated by the Sierra Leone
River. Finally, about a half hour later, gripping my suitcase, I
stepped off the ferry and a young woman called out to me. Nina
de Vries, a Canadian reporter turned media trainer for JHR.
She drove me to my hotel, a dilapidated two-storey structure with
what looked like a bar-restaurant attached to it. People were
hanging around outside. Nina told me to call her when I had
settled in so I could meet the rest of the group. I went to check
in and a male clerk gave me a single key and pointed to the
ramshackle stairs to the left of where we were standing. I looked
at the room number on the key and started to make my way.

You know that feeling you get when you know you're being
watched? I felt that right away. I also felt fear. Something told
me to run. And I did. I tore up those steps while managing to
carry my suitcase. I could hear footsteps coming behind me.
I didn't turn around. I just kept going. I managed to open the
door. Slam it. Lock it. The footsteps came to a halt outside my
door. I was shaking. Would someone burst through? It seemed
like an eternity, but I finally heard the person leave—the sound
of boots fading as they trudged down the hall away from me. I
called Nina. I told her what happened and asked that she and
the others come to get me. I didn't leave the room—they came
upstairs and accompanied me to a waiting car. I called Lloyd
back home and he called the JHR office and asked that I be
moved to a different hotel immediately. I was—and was thank-
ful. At least I felt safe and could start my work.

That work started in a hospital. The big story was maternal mortality. Sierra Leone had the highest maternal death rate in the world. *Time* magazine was in Freetown at the same time as I was doing a special feature on why, in Sierra Leone, death often followed birth. One in seventeen mothers were dying giving life to their child. Nina was mentoring a young reporter and together they were working on a story about the issue. I went with them to the main hospital in Freetown. As soon as we walked through the doors, I understood that death has a smell. Anguish has a smell. Hopelessness has a smell. I could also hear screams. People in pain. The head of the hospital—a doctor who looked exhausted, frustrated—explained to us that the women in this part of the hospital, many of them lying on the floor with only a piece of cloth underneath them, didn't have the means to pay for a private room. This was a shared space. He said that there weren't enough medical staff—doctors, nurses, attendants—to care for them all. The electricity would come and go. Lights would flicker—sometimes during surgeries—and he would be forced to use his rusty flashlight to try to do his job. We went upstairs to the private area, a group of rooms with one or two pregnant women in each. Still not great conditions—but better than what we had seen.

We thanked that doctor and left. There was silence as the three of us drove to the minister of health's office. He was our next interview. After our mentee had asked her questions, I posed a few of my own. I asked the minister, a medical doctor by trade, whether he had thought of rolling up his sleeves and helping out in the hospital we had just left. The situation is dire, as you know, I added. They don't have enough doctors. People are dying. He couldn't get us out of his office soon enough. I guess that was a no.

Another day, the JHR team and I visited a neighbourhood where kids were playing in dirty water. They were dipping their dolls in it. Splashing in it. I was taken by their smiles. Their beauty. Their ability to see good in what I saw as a bad situation. I thought of Blaize at home in Toronto. She had more than enough to eat and drink. Clothes on her back. A house for shelter. These kids didn't have any of those things and yet they smiled. Someone in our group asked the kids to sing their favourite song. They broke out into a version of the ABC song, but to the tune of "Auld Lang Syne." It was beautiful. We clapped for them. They smiled and we smiled back.

At the end of the week, I met with a group of female reporters at JHR's Freetown office. I wanted to hear what life was like for them, how they did their jobs, the challenges they faced. One by one, they told me stories of having to prove themselves, their abilities and their dedication to the job. One reporter shared that her editor refused to give her stories that would keep her at the office late, saying that she needed to be at home to cook for her husband. Another talked about her husband not supporting her media job. "What do you need to work for? Your job is to take care of me!" Others feared retribution. What would happen if they continued to call out government inaction? Human rights abuses? Would they themselves be targeted? I have to admit, I didn't have any answers. What could I say? How could I fix this?

All I could do was listen and record their concerns, encourage them to keep going and tell them how much I respected their passion and courage—because I did.

I want to go back to Sierra Leone one day to see what it's like now, more than ten years later. How it's changed or not changed. I can tell you this: going there changed me. Hearing those young reporters tell their stories, wanting to do their job well, to dig, to uncover the truth even though they could face repercussions, and seeing those children smile, in circumstances that you'd think would make most people cry, taught me something. Hope is bigger than fear. It snuffs it out. Hope is also contagious, and when it spreads, it can bring lasting change.

Two is better than one

Blaize was seven, and she was clear about what she wanted. A brother. Full stop. I didn't think about the echo back to my sister at that very same age, asking my parents for a sister. What I thought instead was, *Boy, that's a promise I can't keep.* Blaize's thinking was, if she was going to give up her single-kid status, she wanted to be the only girl.

It had clearly taken me a while to come around to the possibility of trying to have a second child after Blaize. I was busy with her; I was happy with her. I was content. But I thought about my sister and our relationship and about Blaize being without a sibling. I began to think: maybe two is better.

Lloyd was clear, too, however. He looked at his business, and his schedule, including travel, and he said to me, "You will probably bear the brunt. It really is up to you." OK. Fine. My decision, then. I decided to take the leap. But I was forty years old, so it wasn't a given that Blaize would get a sibling at all, girl or boy. Each month, when my period began, I believed less and less that anything would happen. Until it did.

I didn't tell anyone at work at first, thinking that was the best way to go. Play it safe. Get through that first trimester and then go public. During that time of keeping the news under wraps, Lloyd and I, as we did every September, were planning a trip. We were going away for a few days to celebrate our anniversary. In previous years, we'd visited much of the West Indies. We'd been to Cuba, the Dominican Republic. We'd flown to Argentina. Paris. This year we'd chosen San Francisco, a place neither of us had ever been.

I had a medical checkup scheduled the day before we were to head out of town. I knew something was wrong when the ultrasound technician seemed to go over a certain spot on my stomach numerous times with the wand. I didn't like the look on her face. She told me I could get dressed then disappeared from the tiny room we were in. When she returned, she announced that my pregnancy was nonviable. Nonviable. Such a cold word. Like we were talking about a science experiment. This would have been my child. It was terrible. I was screaming on the inside, crying on the outside.

I looked at Lloyd. Read his face. No answers. What could he say?

We were told that, after we came back from our trip, they would do another ultrasound, to be sure. Then I would have the choice of taking a pill to induce a miscarriage at home or having a procedure in the hospital, a dilation and curettage

(D&C). I already knew my answer to that. There was no way I was taking a pill and waiting for this "nonviable" pregnancy to terminate at home.

We left. Got into the car. Silence on the way home. Lloyd didn't know what to do. How to comfort me. How to make this better. There *was* no making it better.

We headed to San Francisco the next morning, as planned. It's a beautiful city, a walking city. We walked and walked amid the city's trademark cable cars and skyscrapers. The famed Golden Gate Bridge, which we've all seen in photographs and films, was strangely real, right there before us. We ate delicious food and explored Union Square, the waterfront and America's oldest Chinatown. I felt empty, though, but for a bad feeling in the pit of my stomach. Things were not good.

Back in Toronto, a new ultrasound confirmed the results of the first. I was scheduled for the D&C the following day. That meant letting my boss know what was going on. She was supportive. As were my co-hosts. Jeff Hutcheson's wife, Heather, emailed a beautiful letter sharing her own loss. "You will be OK," she said. "This is a club that nobody wants to belong to. But so many of us do."

She was so right. I told a few people and was surprised how many started sharing their stories. How many had experienced the same thing. Who knew? It's not something people normally want to talk about openly. There's a certain shame. A sense of blame. Did I do something wrong? Is there something wrong with me? Why can't I have a healthy child? All these questions went through my mind. Being forty didn't help, either.

Actually, I was closing in on forty-one. If I wanted to give this another shot, time was of the essence. I didn't think there was really much chance. My friend Karen thought otherwise and recommended a fertility doctor named Marjorie Dixon, who's now one of the foremost fertility doctors in the country. Karen said to me, "Marci, it's not about fertility treatment yet. Go in. Come up with a plan. See where you're at." She was right. Dr. Dixon (who has since become a friend) told me my egg health was fine; I just didn't have a whole lot of them. "So let's look at your cycle and try to time things for when you're ovulating." So that's what we did. Strategy first before drugs or anything more drastic.

A couple of months later, I was away at a spa in Tucson, Arizona. (It's one of my favourite spots to go, a place I discovered watching *Oprah* in 2006.) I got what seemed like a really weird period. At the wrong time of the month—about two weeks out. And more like spotting. I knew that could be a sign of something. I was in a "no cell" zone in this spa. Everybody's supposed to be Zen. But I needed to call Dr. Dixon. I couldn't get a signal in my room, so I headed outside, into the desert. I finally got through. She said, "That sounds interesting. When you get back, come straight in for some blood work."

A couple days later, the blood work confirmed I was pregnant. I was stunned.

This pregnancy was a little rougher than my first. It took a bit of a toll. I grew huge and was often tired. I was seven years older, after all. Six months in, I was at work doing a news update on the air. The prompter went blurry. I fumbled through then went and called my obstetrician—the same doctor who'd delivered Blaize. I went in for an appointment that afternoon and described what had happened. He immediately prescribed bed rest. "We are going to move forward with an abundance of caution," he said. It was partly my age and the risk of gestational diabetes and partly my workload and the early hours. I wasn't sleeping well. He thought it was too much.

So that was it. No going back to work. I should have been continuing to anchor the news for another two and a half months. But that was no longer in the cards. My maternity leave would start exactly now.

I braced myself for ten weeks of caution and worry. I would *not* lose this child. I was determined. I was all in now—to this family growing, to the idea that, for us, two kids were definitely better than one. With every passing week, the likelihood of making it to term grew. I felt optimistic, hopeful. While missing the bustle of work and wondering what was in store, I comforted myself by thinking of the longer maternity leave I'd planned for this time around. I would take fourteen months off work and dedicate my time to my kids. Blaize had been an only child for seven years, and I wanted to be there to help her adjust. I wanted to spend all the time I could with the new baby, too. I knew that bouncing back would be harder this time. I was older. Plain and simple. So I stuck to the bed-rest order as faithfully as I could, cherishing those last weeks with Blaize on her own and imagining the rich, busy days to come.

Dash, me and CTV

What is it they say about best-laid plans? Dash was two months old when the president of CTV News, Wendy Freeman, asked to come over for a visit.

Before we get to the surprise outcome of that visit, though, let me back up. Dash and I had been having an amazing time together. He was a newborn, and so my day, of course, was broken into the chunks that correspond to a newborn's schedule: eating, sleeping, changing, sleeping, eating, and so on. There were midnight feedings, but I wasn't going to work in the morning. I enjoyed the time we had together. I'd slip into the guest room with him and watch reality TV in the middle of the night while he fed. I'd get Blaize off to school in the morning, and then Dash and I would go for long walks. We hung out with friends and family. There were lunch dates. Visitors. Naps. I remember standing in school gyms with Dash strapped onto me as I watched my nieces compete at sports.

Time slows when you have a newborn. Or it vanishes. I'd fallen into a different world, a whole new life. So when I look back, it was surprising to realize Dash was only around a month old when Lis Travers, executive producer of *Canada AM*, got in touch and asked if she could come by. When she arrived, we sat down together in our living room. I was holding Dash as he slept. Then we had what felt to me like a very strange conversation. At first, I didn't understand what she was trying to tell me. She had trouble getting the words out. The gist of it was that CTV was dealing with serious cutbacks. Every department had to tighten. In the case of *Canada AM*, in order to meet the new budget, my newscast would be eliminated, or at least me reading it.

Here's how the show worked. Normally, the co-hosts would open the show. Then they'd throw to the news anchor—that was me, and had been for eight years, since 2003—for the headline package, which would include all the major and breaking news with, perhaps, some short interviews woven in with reporters in the field. The news anchor (again, me) would throw back to the main desk. The co-hosts would then take over to conduct the lengthier interviews, some delving deeper into the headlines and others more like features on broader topics. With my position eliminated, the two co-hosts would instead simply take turns reading the news headlines at the beginning of each half hour.

That was the plan. By sacrificing me and my position, the show would be on budget. I was the only one to be cut.

Lis assured me there would be a position for me with the network when I returned from my maternity leave. She mentioned CTV News Channel as a possibility; she mentioned something else. There was no clarity. Don't worry, she said, there'll be a job.

But I was deeply offended. I was hurt. I'd been with *Canada AM* for more than ten years, and now I was suddenly out, drifting, and they would somehow find a job for me? I felt completely disrespected. I quickly decided I wasn't going back and that I wouldn't let the powers that be at the network choose my destiny.

It was Thanksgiving weekend. I went into the *Canada* AM offices knowing that there wouldn't be many people in and cleared out my desk.

Meanwhile, my co-workers and I had been planning to get together so they could meet Dash. The show's co-hosts, Seamus O'Regan and Beverly Thompson, as well as Jeff Hutcheson, the weather and sports anchor, came for lunch one afternoon. It was pleasant, friendly and great to see them. I didn't mention my visit from our boss. And none of them brought up the fact that I was no longer on the show. This was a social call. We didn't go there. We talked about babies, about life.

In the days that followed, I began making phone calls, considering my future, pondering what direction my career might take post-CTV.

Then, a couple of weeks later, Seamus called. He wanted to tell me he was planning to leave *Canada AM* to become a correspondent for the national news. He'd been co-hosting *Canada* AM for nine years, and he felt it was an important step to do some reporting out in the field to round out his experience.

I said, "But Seamus, you've interviewed everyone." It was true, he had, from prime ministers to presidents and everything in between. "What does it matter where you interviewed them, on a morning show or on Parliament Hill?" But he'd made up his mind.

That left Seamus's co-hosting seat on *Canada AM* vacant. Of course everyone and their mother had ideas about who would replace him. No one expected it to be a woman. Since its inception in 1972, the show had been hosted by a male-female team.

It wasn't long after hearing from Seamus that I received that call from Wendy Freeman. We arranged a time for her to come by. It was quite the parade of visitors Dash and I had during those few weeks! I was cradling him in one arm as I answered the door. I brought her in, and we settled on the couch with cups of tea. Wendy got right to the chase. She told me she thought the best man for the job was a woman. She offered me the position. I was in shock. I had not seen this coming.

A couple of weeks before, I'd been discarded. Or that was how, to me, it had appeared; that was what had happened, as far as I could tell. Who knew what was going on behind the scenes? Nobody told me whether this was the plan all along. All I knew was that I'd been turning my attention to making a serious shift in my career after my maternity leave. Suddenly being offered one of the most significant news chairs in the country wasn't part of that plan.

But I wanted it, and I told Wendy just that. I would be the first Black woman in Canada to co-host a national morning show. Bev and I would be the first female team. We would, as had been the plan when my news anchor position was cut, take turns reporting the news headlines every half hour during the show. We'd continue to work alongside Jeff, who'd be staying on in sports and weather.

There was a trade-off to this good news, however, and it was significant. The network wanted to launch the show in its new incarnation early in the new year. That meant going back to work in January, several months before I had planned. I asked for more time, but they wouldn't bend. They were set. I knew what this microphone being offered to me meant, and I wanted it. I'd be making history, and I felt it was important to take this job and do it well. I couldn't squander this opportunity.

But I was sad. I'd regretted having so little time off with Blaize after she was born. I'd been determined not to do that again. Yet here I was. Taking less time at home with Dash as a baby was a huge sacrifice to make. By now I was no stranger to moments like this in my career. Moments where I was asked—no, *required*—to leap, come what may. Where I had to go forward even if it meant letting something go—including something that mattered as much as time off work with my newborn son.

So I resigned myself to the compromise and got a childcare plan in place.

"What did you have?"

The piano was set. The lighting was great. Cameras were ready. There came a knock on the hotel room door. Trish, our producer, opened it.

And in walked Lionel Richie.

It's a moment I won't forget. I was just heading back to work after my shortened maternity leave with Dash. Blaize, in grade two, was a proud big sister. She'd gotten just what she'd asked for—a baby brother—and had immediately become his fierce protector. In the hospital, after he was born, she was given a wristband that said "Big Sister." Her stuffed bear, Danny, also had a wristband. I had a band, and, of course, so did Dash, though he didn't yet have a name. He was just "Baby Exeter." Blaize wanted us to name him Awesome. At home, she was delighted, engaged, cute. She held him so carefully. It was wonderful to watch her as she took on her new role in the family.

Letting go of those wide-open days of mothering to return to work was hard. But I have to confess, it helped ease the anguish a little when I learned that my first taped interview as co-host of *Canada AM* was to be with Lionel Richie.

What luck! Though of course it's not supposed to matter when you're a journalist conducting an interview—just as teachers aren't meant to have favourite students—I was a big fan. I'd met Lionel once in the past, but briefly, accidentally, way back, before Blaize had been born, in what now seemed a different life.

Trish and I had decided we wanted atmosphere for this interview, so we'd booked a room in a downtown hotel and asked if a piano could be placed in it. Lionel was promoting his new album *Tuskegee*, which was named after his hometown in Alabama. When he walked in, he stopped to shake hands with all the crew members. He got to me last.

"Hi!" He smiled broadly. "What did you have?"

I stared at him, open-mouthed. I couldn't believe it.

Back up seven whole years. Late spring 2004. I was seven months pregnant with Blaize and doing double duty at work. In the early mornings, I anchored the *Canada AM* newscast, reading the news at the top and bottom of each hour, starting at six. Normally the news anchor would sign off with the hosts at the end of the show at nine. But I would leave right after reading the eight thirty news and cross the hall to anchor a three-hour show on CTV News Channel. Often during that show, I'd follow up with reporters about news that was breaking during *Canada AM*, cut to live events such as political press conferences, and conduct more in-depth interviews with expert guests on issues related to current events. It was an unforgiving schedule, exhausting at the best of times, and increasingly so as my pregnancy progressed. I was lucky that I had no complications and felt healthy and strong.

One morning, I'd finished my final newscast on *Canada AM* and was getting my makeup touched up during a commercial break before heading over to News Channel. My original makeup would have been applied hours earlier. Often during that half-hour ritual, *Canada AM* producers would pop in to chat about the morning's guests, anything I needed to know about a segment we'd planned, potential stories.

No time for that now, though, between shows. This was just a quick refresher. Weather anchor Tom Brown was in the next chair getting his own makeup done. The makeup artist with me was deftly powdering my nose when in walked Lionel Richie. By himself. No entourage. Just him. He was a guest on the show that morning and was due on-air very shortly. He plunked down in the hair chair; nobody was there—the morning shows' hair dresser had gone for the day. Lionel introduced himself and shook hands with everyone in the room one by one. He noticed my tummy.

"Hi," he said, greeting me like an old friend. "How are you doing?"

"I'm fine, Lionel," I said. "It's such a pleasure to meet you.

I'm a news anchor on the show you're about to sing on. But I also do another show, so I have to miss your performance."

"Best of luck with the baby," he said.

"Thank you!"

Tom grabbed his phone and asked if he could take a picture of Lionel and me. I silently thanked him. He knew I was a fan. We posed—*click!*—and I walked over to News Channel, thinking about how kind Lionel had seemed. How humble. How he apparently preferred to hang out with us in the makeup room instead of in the solitude of an assigned green room. He wanted to be among us.

There are people who become celebrities for two minutes and then want only red jelly beans and white flowers, and nobody better disturb them. They've got riders; they're demanding God knows what—that everything must be two centimetres apart, it sometimes feels like. Not Lionel. Nor Tony Bennett, who, when he'd come on the show, had addressed every camera operator and asked how they were doing. Kenny Rogers, too. He'd once been booked to appear on *Canada AM* the morning after performing at Casino Rama, an hour and thirty minutes north of Toronto. He'd driven down with his team the night before, and they'd all slept right there in the parking lot, on their bus, so they could be up first thing to haul out their equipment for his early-morning appearance. We're talking Kenny Rogers, sleeping in a parking lot.

Someone once said to me, "The bigger they are, the more humble they are." That, to me, is the true definition of a pro.

That photo of me and Lionel in the makeup room is the only one I have of me pregnant with Blaize. For the longest time, Blaize thought the man in the picture was an old family friend. She had no idea who he was. I suspect that would make Lionel smile.

A lifetime later, greeting Lionel in the hotel room we'd set up for our interview, I gathered myself, got over my shock, and said, "A girl. I had a girl after you saw me."

"Congratulations."

"But I just had a boy. He's four months old."

"Oh my goodness," he said. "Every time I see you, you're having babies!"

I laughed and shook his hand. "So good to see you. We thought we could do our interview sitting at the piano."

"Sounds great."

We sat down.

Often, for a celebrity interview, a publicist will insist that certain questions aren't asked and that the conversation be limited to whatever is being promoted. The publicist will stress that the current project—be it a book, an album, a film—is the only subject allowed—the only topic to be covered. Sometimes, a journalist's (and by extension, a show's) "access" to such an artist is granted on the basis that such parameters will be respected. If you don't adhere, if you pose an unwelcome question, enter forbidden territory—say, something controversial or personal—you might have a hard time securing an interview with this person in the future. It's an uncomfortable situation for a journalist with any kind of integrity, but when the interview is important, you make the deal and find subtle ways, in your interview, to work around it as best you can: to still conduct a meaningful interview that is more than just a publicity opportunity for the artist, a conversation that contains something of substance, something fresh.

Lionel said to ask him anything. He was willing to talk about whatever I wanted to talk about. So we talked about civil rights. About his growing up in Tuskegee, where he was surrounded by Black professionals—where he had examples of Black excellence all around him, as I had noticed and been bowled over by as a child on my first trip to Jamaica. We spoke about how he'd briefly thought about becoming a priest but had pursued music instead. How he had deep regrets about relationships and the way he'd handled himself in certain situations. How after a life on the road, he was now trying to make up time with his kids and grandkids: to be more present.

It wasn't an interview. It was a conversation. Two people connecting on life, love and growth. At the end of it, I asked Lionel if he would play a song for me. "Easy." One of the Commodores' greatest hits. "Sure," he said.

His fingers tapped the keys, and I melted.

There I was, side by side on a piano bench with Lionel Richie. And he was playing my favourite song. For me, it seemed, and for my kids.

Lionel Richie and me. I'm seven months pregnant with Blaize.

The everything show

My first day co-hosting on *Canada AM*, they had me come out from behind a curtain. It was a game of surprise for our viewers. They gave hints: This person played hockey. This person did a kids' show. I sashayed out to Michael Jackson's "Wanna Be Startin' Somethin'."

People wrote in with congratulations. Some said, "We were hoping it would be you." It was lovely. We did a little press tour and were featured in media like *Starweek* magazine. It was a new era for this iconic show: Bev and I would be the first pair of women to sit at that desk together.

It was also a new "era" for my career. As the three main faces of *Canada AM*, Bev, Jeff and I would spend more time with each other over the next four years than with our own families.

I took my role and the position I'd been offered—the

privilege and opportunity of my microphone—very seriously. It was something I didn't want to take for granted. I wanted to be so good: to be really well prepared for each segement, to ask the questions that would bring the story forward. As a program in the tradition of morning shows like NBC's *The Today Show* or ABC's *Good Morning America, Canada AM* was an immense undertaking. Three hours of live television every single day, it was part serious journalism, part politics and breaking news, part lifestyle and entertainment. It was everything in one morning, five mornings per week. We were cooking one minute and interviewing the prime minister the next.

Well, not quite in that order. The first half of the program was dedicated to hard news, and then the show would get lighter and less intense. By the time the third hour came along, we could be doing anything. This was when our musical guests appeared. Sometimes we had a studio audience, sometimes not. We might have someone teaching us how to do something: an aerobics instructor, a dance instructor. People got married on *Canada AM*. We did a kitchen party on a patio we had as part of our set. We had a food truck drive up and we did taste tests on the air.

But we also reported on the gravest news and most urgent issues our country was facing at any given time. Bev and I alternated reporting the lead story each morning, and likewise switched off on the segments that followed. When you've conducted years of interviews with officials and experts on dozens of incidents and topics, on matters of importance to various communities or constituencies, and often to the country as a whole, it's remarkable to look back and find that they don't all blur together; in fact, a significant number of the stories and segments remain clear in your memory, as if they took place only last week.

One of these, for me, is an interview I did with Chuck Strahl, an MP and cabinet minister in Stephen Harper's Conservative government, who was in charge of what is now called Indigenous and Northern Affairs. We'd been reporting on the large number of long-lasting boil-water advisories in many First Nations communities, and this interview was about ongoing issues at a particular reserve that didn't have safe drinking water. I had a *Canada AM* mug on the desk. During the interview I picked it up, took a swig of water and said it was disgraceful that Indigenous people in this country couldn't do what I'd just done with confidence. It was dramatic. It was a bit of grandstanding. But I wanted to get the point across. I asked the minister why it was OK that people couldn't give a glass of water to their kids and be sure they wouldn't get sick. He went into this whole thing about how the current government was no worse than the previous government. I lost it. I said, "I don't think Canadians want to know what the previous government did or didn't do. They want to know what you're doing."

It was quite a confrontational interview. I'm proud of it. I don't know whether it made a difference, but at least if there were any First Nations people watching, they felt seen. And for the people who weren't First Nations, they would have understood clearly that they had things they took for granted—clean water, food, emergency workers at the ready when needed—that the people who founded this country, who were here first, don't have.

It was a bit of a history lesson that morning. I loved that interview. It's an example of what I hoped to accomplish on that show. I wanted to draw the audience right in and have the interviewee address them—all the people at home watching, people getting ready for work, gulping down their breakfasts, getting ready to herd their kids out the door. I'd often say, especially to politicians, "What would you like to say to Canadians right now? What aren't Canadians understanding, in your opinion?"

I didn't want to ever have to change who I was as a person while in that role. I wanted to stay true to myself. To do that, I aimed to be true to the people who were watching.

The art of listening

It would be easy to think a television news host's chief skill lies in asking questions: she wants, consistently, to pose the right question, in the right way, at the right time. To, at each point in an interview, bring up the query that's arising in the viewer's mind. This is the standard you aim for when you're the co-host of a national morning show.

But if, during an interview, you are so focused on your next question that you're only half taking in what your guest is saying, and therefore failing to respond when something they've said begs a response—a key question you hadn't planned to ask or simply some natural reaction on your part—the interview will feel stilted. It might even stall. Your subject won't be at ease and won't speak openly.

When interviewing politicians and people in power, you hope to steer them from their talking points or "message" and move the conversation past politics. This can happen through pressure and tough questions: you may want such a guest thrown off balance (such as when I interviewed Chuck Strahl, as I described in the last chapter). But other times, a more natural conversation may lead even the most astute politician to speak more plainly and frankly than they had planned. Natural means listening. *Actually* listening, even as you keep your list of important questions in mind. It's a delicate balance the best interviewers learn to maintain.

And for those interviews that lean more toward human interest, if you aren't slowing down to really hear what your guest is saying, you wind up with an uncomfortable interviewee. Such a guest won't offer much to engage your audience because you aren't giving them that safe space in which a conversation— and, by extension, a good interview—can blossom. They can't just be themselves.

There are other situations, though, when listening is not only an important interviewing skill but the only thing you can do.

In late 2014, nearly two years after the tragic school shooting at Sandy Hook Elementary School in Newtown, Connecticut, I interviewed Scarlett Lewis on *Canada AM*. Her six-year-old son, Jesse, had died that day at Sandy Hook. The gunman had come into his classroom and paused to reload. Jesse screamed at his classmates, "Run! Run!" Some of them did. At age six, he had the impulse and presence of mind to shout for his classmates to get out. He saved several kids' lives that day.

Jesse's mother had since set up a foundation in Jesse's name to advocate for social and emotional education in schools. Her book, *Nurturing Healing Love: A Mother's Journey of Hope and Forgiveness*, had just been published. I talked to her via satellite. The first question I asked her was "How do you move forward?"

She said you don't forget, but in order to move on, you have to find a place where you can forgive; otherwise, you're paralyzed. She didn't think it would be honouring her son if she just lay down and didn't fight and speak up. She said you have to get to a point where you forgive in your own way. Her book was named after a phrase Jesse had written on the chalkboard in their kitchen not long before he died: nurturing healing love. She felt it was her mission to continue to fight for empathy in his memory. Her son, she said, had taught her so much.

I couldn't believe she could formulate words and answer the questions I was asking her after losing her son the way she had. I just didn't get it. That's when you know someone is on a higher plane. They're just operating in a different dimension. This woman was devastated. She'd lost her everything, and now she's putting her everything into changing things, making things better. She's pivoting to forgiveness. That's the hardest thing to do.

No one would have blamed Scarlett Lewis if she'd just disappeared and we never heard her name again—if she quietly, privately, mourned her son for the rest of her life. But she wanted to make sure her son's short life had made a difference. And she was going to do that through her foundation's work, her writing, through speaking in public. Putting herself through interviews like this one.

You don't learn, as a host, to do an interview like that. Your job is to listen. I had read her book to prepare, but you have to be careful not to over-prepare. You have to enter a hyper-listening state so that you don't miss a single word and the person knows you're locked in.

She was comfortable,
I was comfortable

The first time I spoke with journalist Amanda Lindhout was via satellite, shortly after her release following fifteen months of captivity in Somalia, where she had been kidnapped by Islamist insurgents in August 2008 while attempting to visit an internally displaced persons camp to conduct interviews alongside Australian photojournalist Nigel Brennan. She was very fragile, having endured several months of brutal treatment, including torture and serial rape.

We met in person four years later, upon the release of her memoir, *A House in the Sky*, which she co-wrote with journalist Sara Corbett. I sat her down and said, "Listen, we are not going to be discussing anything you don't want to discuss. If you're uncomfortable with something, we just move on. You tell your story as you see fit." I believe I was holding her hand during the countdown before the cameras came up. I'd told her, "Don't worry about the cameras around you. You're just talking to me."

We weren't friends, not at that time, not yet. But she had already impressed me in so many ways. When Amanda had gone to Somalia, she was a relatively inexperienced foreign correspondent trying to gain experience and build a career. She'd briefly reported from Iraq and Afghanistan, but her only professional affiliation while in Somalia was with the *Red Deer Advocate* in Alberta. Before heading to Kabul, she'd worked as a cocktail waitress. She'd had no formal training. When the news of her abduction broke, many journalists, some of my colleagues among them, were more critical than sympathetic, saying, "Why was she there? She knew it was dangerous." And, it was implied, and sometimes said outright, she wasn't even the real thing, a proper journalist. She hadn't studied or paid her dues.

It wasn't my instinct to blame Amanda for her own misfortune or to question her motives. After all, a hankering for adventure and a certain recklessness aren't uncommon among foreign correspondents. And besides, it's not as if experienced journalists are immune from being targeted by insurgents and kidnappers or incapable of mistakes or bad luck. NBC foreign correspondent Richard Engel has written in his own memoir, *A Fist in the Hornet's Nest*, of the "bravado, gumption and good luck" that saw him through his early years in the business, including an early foray into Cairo with no knowledge of Arabic, no local contacts, no journalistic affiliation, "and no real clue what I was getting myself into." Had Amanda been more reckless than he had been? Or was such reckless bravado less appealing, less admirable, in an attractive former cocktail waitress than in a rugged male college graduate?

There's a real pettiness sometimes in journalism circles. I didn't see Amanda as some trifling young woman who got herself into a situation she shouldn't have been in. I didn't think, *You know Somalia's the most dangerous place on earth. Why in God's name would you go there? And then the Canadian government's supposed to get you out?* No. I admired Amanda tremendously. She was warm. She was real. Warts and all. When you read her story, you understand the poverty she came from. Her education was through books and reading, and *National Geographic* magazine was her main source material. She had the courage to go. She was trying to understand what was going on in Somalia. If we don't have people go into such areas—people who are running in when everyone else is running out—we will never get the real story. That's what she was trying to do: shine a light on stories that the world wasn't really seeing. It's important to see those dark corners. She wasn't afraid to tell it like it is, and she's one of those people who stands up for the little guy, even though she's the little guy. I appreciated that. I appreciated her heart. Her curiosity. And her capacity to forgive. She's a survivor of terrible cruelty, but she'll say, "I understand why those boys did what they did to me." I really respected her.

After our interview, her publicist came to me and said, "Amanda feels really comfortable with you." They had some events coming up as part of her promotional tour, and she wondered whether I would interview her at Indigo and a couple of other places. I said yes. She was comfortable, I was comfortable.

After that, we kept in touch. We'd talk on the phone. She'd call me with story ideas. We spoke after the news broke that one of the men responsible for her kidnapping had been arrested in Ottawa. She was to give an impact statement but was overwhelmed by the prospect of facing him in court. She asked if I would come. I took the day off work and flew to Ottawa. When she came into the courtroom, she was bawling. She saw me and came over to where I was seated. I held her. She gave her impact statement while looking at that man, who had been the translator for the group that had held her. We stayed in Ottawa that night, met for dinner, talked.

Amanda is one of those friends I don't have to talk to every day, but I know that the next time I do, we'll pick up where we left off. Our conversations these days focus on her healing, her recovery and her immense growth. I'm so proud of her. I love her very much. There's this West Indian saying about how like attracts like. I recognize something in Amanda. When you have a certain mindset, a creed that you live by, and you encounter someone with similar leanings, something happens. There's a spark. But it's not just that. There was something else there, too. She trusted me with her story. She trusted me at a time when she felt really vulnerable. I didn't take that lightly. And I never took that for granted.

Amanda Lindhout and me, just after an interview on *The Social*.

The coach

I love sports documentaries. ESPN does them well. Those *30 for 30* films are the best. You don't have to love sports to love a good story: "Into the Wind," directed by Canadian NBA legend Steve Nash, covers Terry Fox and his heroic Marathon of Hope; "Celtics/Lakers: Best of Enemies" captures moments beyond the infamous Larry Bird–Magic Johnson rivalry; and "O.J.: Made in America," which won an Academy Award for best documentary, does a deep dive into race and celebrity, putting under the microscope Simpson's life, his NFL career and the trial of the century.

I was always looking for different projects or stories to work on outside of my news anchor duties on *Canada AM*. After getting some new numbers (which in TV speak means ratings or information on demographics), we learned that of all the specialty channels, TSN (Canada's sports channel) was the channel that *Canada AM* watchers viewed the most. So, simply put, if you watched TSN, you were also likely to tune in to us in the mornings. That was a huge lightbulb moment for me. Jeff Hutcheson, our sports anchor, did a great job of bringing highlights and interesting stories to our viewers, but we didn't often do longer pieces on a sports theme. What if *Canada AM* and TSN worked together to produce a piece that could live on both platforms?

It was basketball season—the Toronto Raptors were rolling—and Kyle Lowry, the team's starting point guard, was having a stellar season. He would make a fantastic subject.

Full of grit and a superior basketball IQ, Kyle was from North Philadelphia and had been a star at Villanova University. He'd played a couple of seasons in Memphis for the Grizzlies and in Houston for the Rockets—but with the Raptors, he had found a home. I approached my bosses, pointing to the numbers and the connection between our show and sports fans. It took some prodding (I have to admit I was relentless), but I was given approval, as well as an award-winning TSN producer named Craig Chambers to work with. I contacted the Raptors' then-director of media relations, Jim LaBumbard, to ask what the chances were of getting Kyle to talk to us. Jim explained that ESPN was already working on a similar piece. Me versus ESPN. I thought not.

· · ·

We needed another subject. Another strong subject. So we turned to the man Kyle would later call "one of the best coaches I've ever had": Dwane Casey. I had met Coach Casey once before, during a quick interview a couple of years back on Martin Luther King Jr.'s birthday. Casey had been raised in the Deep South of the United States, and he offered his thoughts on the importance of King and his fight for racial equality. I'd watched him patrol the sidelines for years while going to games with my dad. He was no-nonsense. He wasn't shy about letting referees know he disagreed with a call (in his trademark hoarse voice) or calling out to players on the court.

I called Jim again. He called back with great news. The coach was available. We set a date for the interview: Easter Monday, April 6, 2015. I started my research and was intrigued by his story: He grew up in Morganfield, Kentucky, population 3,400. He attended a high school called Union County and would sometimes, on his way to morning classes, have to bypass members of the Ku Klux Klan marching outside. Integration was underway in the South, but not everyone was happy about it. By the time high-school graduation rolled around, he was a highly coveted recruit and chose the University of Kentucky. There he was a star point guard and helped guide the 1977–1978 Wildcats team to an NCAA championship. He spent four years at Kentucky earning a degree in business administration. In 1979, his coach, Joe B. Hall, offered him an assistant coaching position. A career was born.

Meanwhile, Craig was working the NBA side of Casey's story and had managed to get an interview with former Seattle Supersonics head coach George Karl. Casey had been Karl's assistant. We wanted to get his take on Casey's coaching style and what made him an integral part of Karl's system. Our plan was to hand Casey an iPad during our interview so he could watch what Karl had said about him. We wanted to see his immediate reaction. Craig was also able to collect some great family photos. In one of them, Casey was dressed in a gingham shirt and sported a serious Afro. Another was a group photo of Casey in his high-school choir. We had lovely video of his family as well. It was all coming together.

The day of our interview arrived, and our crew was setting up at a restaurant close to the former Air Canada Centre. The Raptors had played their last game of the regular season the night before (a loss) and an end-of-season press conference was just wrapping up. We wanted to be in a different location because we wanted a more intimate set-up and needed more interview time. I could see Coach Casey and Jim walking through the doors. The coach didn't look particularly happy. He was likely wondering why he had to do one more interview when he had playoffs to prepare for. Why this interview was separate from the others. Craig and I greeted them and introduced them to the rest of our crew. While lights were being adjusted, I made small talk, asking about the previous night's game and the upcoming playoffs. The shop talk improved his mood. He relaxed. Craig gave us the green light and we started.

Casey told us about his childhood. How his grandparents had raised him. How in the summers he worked different jobs, including tobacco farming and coal mining. He told us about having to get takeout food at the back of the local chicken restaurant because Blacks weren't allowed to walk through the front door. He told us that, through all the pain, frustration and fear that segregation caused, he had a plan. And he stuck to it. High school. University. Basketball. Midway through the conversation, I pulled the iPad out, pressed play and handed it to him. He had just told me how much George Karl had meant to him. How he was a great leader, a fantastic head coach and how much he had learned as his assistant. Then, Casey watched as Karl said essentially the same things about him: that Casey could connect with the players in a way he couldn't. That he was patient. That he was kind. That he was skilled. I saw something then that I hadn't seen in all the years I had observed the coach from afar: a broad smile. It was a great moment.

Weeks later, I would hear a TSN SportsCentre anchor introduce our story: "With more on Coach Casey, here is *Canada AM*'s Marci Ien." It is one of my favourite interviews. It exemplifies a vision coming to fruition, teamwork across several platforms and how research—going that extra mile—pays off.

Fate versus luck

While a prisoner at Auschwitz during the Second World War, Max Eisen suffered a brutal beating by a Nazi guard. He was fifteen. The chief surgeon at the camp took pity on him and asked permission for the teen to work as his assistant. Eisen survived the camp, was liberated in 1945 and came to Canada in 1949, where he settled in Toronto, married and had two children. (He now has several great-grandchildren.) Eisen gives credit for his survival, in part, to the actions of that surgeon, Dr. Tadeusz Orzeszko, who he later learned was a member of the Polish resistance.

Eisen's book, *By Chance Alone: A Remarkable True Story of Courage and Survival at Auschwitz,* won the RBC Taylor Prize in 2017 and CBC's Canada Reads in 2019 (his book was selected by television personality Ziya Tong). When I interviewed Eisen on *Canada AM*, I asked him about the title of his book and that whole idea of chance. I said to him, "What if it wasn't chance at all?"

I meant, what if he was supposed to survive, so he could be here now to tell his story, this incredible human story of perseverance? There he was, he'd lost his family, he'd lost so many loved ones, and people were dying all around him. Yet through the actions of this doctor, who took pity on him and took a risk by speaking up for him, he lives. Eisen's story shines a light on both the worst and the best of human nature. That he is able to share it with the rest of us is huge: it's a piece of living history, a window on the extremes of human nature, and the possibility of finding goodness even in the darkest circumstances.

By suggesting it may have been Eisen's fate to survive, I don't mean that he was more deserving than those who died or that he had more to offer the world. But I often wonder about the idea of fate. It's a fact: we're all going to die at some point, and we're not all going to live a long and leisurely life. Maybe we all come part and parcel with some sort of plan — a predetermined amount of time in which to fulfill what we're supposed to fulfill. Whether we do or not, I don't know. But some of us don't get a decades-long lifetime in which to do it. Some people's stories have fewer chapters than others: some get one chapter; some get ninety.

Eisen's story had a profound effect on me. When he and I spoke about fate versus luck, when I said maybe he was supposed to be here to tell us this story, he listened. He just listened. There I was, the journalist, sharing my own thoughts on-air about the deepest mysteries of existence. It was, briefly, as if the interview had flipped around. That happens. Rarely—as host, you're keenly aware the show isn't meant to be about you—but it can. Your inner self slips in and speaks up. When an interview is real. When it goes places.

Being first

A cold case had been reopened after many years. A little girl had been killed. Those stories are always difficult. Our guest was an investigator who had originally worked on the case. For such an interview, we'd usually talk about the case, what had happened in the past and what new evidence had come to light.

In preparation, I'd also look into the investigating officer's background. I'd want to know some details: What sorts of cases has he worked on before? Is he married? Does he have kids? How old are they? Then I'd be able to ask, "When you're investigating a crime like this, how difficult is it when you have a twelve-year-old at home?" It was about going beyond the badge, beyond the headline, to the person in front of me.

I've taken the time to find out who they are, so I can allow their humanity to come through.

I've always been compelled to dig deeper on stories in this way. To out-research everyone. Ask questions nobody else has asked. It isn't just that I want to do my job well. It isn't just that I have a competitive streak. I did, and I do. But it goes beyond either of those motivations.

I was the first Black woman to host a national morning show in this country. I was part of the first all-women co-hosting team for a national morning show.

When you're first at anything, when you're aware of breaking new ground, you think hard on the responsibility attached to that. When you walk into a room, it's as if you bring an entire community in with you. Sometimes you feel you have a million people on your back. It's not that it's a bad form of pressure. But it *is* pressure, and it's constant. You can't squander this chance. You can't ever underperform or make a mistake, because that mistake might impact someone else being hired.

Nobody told me, when I was hired for *Canada AM*, that I had to be better than everyone else, but I felt it: I had to study harder. I had to be great. There was no room for error. I wanted to make sure that I protected this legacy. That meant being professional at all times, not just in front of the camera, but off it as well: I was representing the network everywhere I went. If I'm in a job like this, I am a role model, so I have to carry myself that way. There are people watching. My decisions are always made, and my work carried out, with that in mind.

When film writer, director and producer Lee Daniels was

in town for the Toronto International Film Festival, I went to the TIFF Bell Lightbox downtown to do an extended interview with him for *Canada AM*. It was a Sunday afternoon, and he was giving a talk that evening. I admired his work. I'd seen many of his films, including *The Butler, Shadowboxer* and *Monster's Ball*, which he'd produced and for which Halle Berry had won an Oscar for best actress in 2002—to this day the only African American woman to win that award. *Precious*, which he directed and co-produced, was one of my favourite movies of all time.

I knew Thursday or Friday that this was coming, so I did a deep dive for a few days. I re-watched the films and researched his life, which was in itself fascinating. Here Daniels was, this gay Black boy whose father was a cop: his father wanted to beat the gay out of him. He'd caught him dressing in women's clothing and beaten him to a pulp. Yet his father had also taught him his love of language, pushed him to read, and made him and his siblings give recitations. So through that father, both a brutal and learned man, he gained really divergent kinds of knowledge at an early age—on the one hand, he experienced cruelty, and on the other, he learned about the beauty of language and a story's ability to raise us above the worst sides of our natures.

When a movie personality is made available for interviews, they are set up in a room and the different media are given time slots. So we were in this little room at the Lightbox. A couple questions in, I told Daniels that given his own life experiences, I had been wondering why he'd never made a film based on his own life. But then, as I was reviewing his films, it had hit me:

there was no need to do an autobiographical film. He'd left bits and pieces of himself in all the films he'd done. He was leaving bread crumbs in all of his work.

Silence. Then he said, "Just stop for a second." Then he said, "Wow, you are so good."

Had Daniels thought of his films this way before? I don't know. (I don't think so.) After that, we just talked. He was amazing. A little eccentric. We spoke about his father. His own trouble with addiction. How, when Berry had won the Oscar, he never made it to the party. I said, "What were you doing?" "Medicating myself," he said. He was that open; it was that kind of interview. We were locked in conversation. We forgot the cameras were there.

The piece was edited that Sunday and ran on our show the next morning. The editor who'd worked on it sent me a note saying how great it was: it was a really special interview, and he'd been honoured to edit it.

That meant so much to me. A note like that could keep me going when the going was hard. It *was* hard, at times. Co-hosting *Canada AM* was a gruelling schedule. And the work environment wasn't always perfect. Whose is? There were times when I thought I'd had enough. Of the hours. The pressure. Maybe I should go back to the idea of teaching. Maybe I should just throw in the towel.

I remember Lloyd saying to me once, "If you don't like it, you should leave."

But I knew in my heart that I couldn't. It was that "being first" thing. That "role model" thing. I told him, "It's not that easy for me. I'm doing something not a lot of people do. I have a responsibility." I wanted to make sure my time spent on that show was intact and full and that I stayed the course.

It's hard to stay the course sometimes.

But then you interview someone like Lee Daniels. You probe an investigator of a cold case brought back to light. You pin down a cabinet minister. You encounter the impossible grace of a survivor of tragedy, such as Max Eisen or Scarlett Lewis. You give your viewers information, answers, moments in which they pause to take something in, thinking, "Wow."

And you know it's worth it.

Less than twenty-four hours in Kentucky

As I write this, Barry Manilow is in Vegas. He's on his *Night Songs II* tour. A glance at his Facebook page tells me he sweeps onto stage to raucous chants of "Barry! Barry! Barry!" Streamers and glow sticks abound.

There was a time, though, not so long ago, when Barry was on the verge of retirement. Officially. In 2015, he embarked on his One Last Time! tour, which just so happened to be forty years after he logged his first number-one hit with "Mandy."

I am a big fan of his. I've been listening to him since I was seven years old. My sister introduced him to me. His old-time music is *my* music. A recent review online gushes that he's "genuine Velveeta. Weapons-grade schmaltz. His veins flow with pure glitter." To which I nod fervently. *Yes.* That's my Barry. I love the whole package: his soothing baritone; that he started out writing jingles; and that he's this scrawny, tiny guy from Brooklyn who doesn't look at all like a musical superstar. When Barry announced this was it, his last tour, I said to myself, "There's no way he can retire and I've not seen him in concert live."

I got online and looked up the schedule. The only concert in his whole tour that I could conceivably attend was on a Friday night in Louisville, Kentucky. The day after the concert, I was hosting my dad's seventy-fifth birthday party at my house. No matter. This was doable. I bought a ticket, booked a flight, arranged for the kids to stay with a friend (because Lloyd was away), took Friday off work and flew, via a connection in Atlanta, to Kentucky.

It was mid-afternoon when I arrived. I checked into the storied Galt House Hotel and stood looking out the window of my hotel room in downtown Louisville. Now, here's the thing about choosing to make something happen, just for yourself— because it's important to you, even if it might look, on the surface, indulgent and unrealistic. I mean, did I really wedge this in between my duties at *Canada AM*, as a mother, and celebrating my dad's silver birthday? A pop concert in another country? Of course I did. I'm not advocating that we all habitually book off work and fly to Kentucky when the mood strikes. But occasionally, we do need to break out of our routines, to make room for those joyous occasions—those that are within our reach. They might be modest; they might be less glittery than me racing off to see Barry Manilow live for the first time in my life. Whatever those breakout moments are, they matter. Because when you fit them in, inevitably, you're making space—not just for the exciting event you've planned, but for the unexpected as well.

Looking out the window of my hotel room, I saw that right across the street was the Muhammad Ali Center, a non-profit museum and cultural space devoted to multiculturalism and to promoting Ali's legacy: his ideals of respect, hope and inspiration. I'd caught an early flight. I was so tired. But I thought, *Oh boy, I have to make time for this. No nap for me.* I changed into a track suit, walked over and toured the building. I read about Ali's life, his family, and pored over exhibits about non-violent change. There were clips of Ali talking before some of his fights, about George Foreman and the Rumble in the Jungle, and about refusing to go to Vietnam and losing his title. Walking through this man's life, virtually, year by year, I felt a connection to him and to the place. It's a warm, special place.

Out in the streets of Louisville afterward, I kept walking and continued my unplanned, contemplative tour. I stopped at historical plaques about events in the civil rights movement, the abolishment of slavery—there was even one with a Canadian connection, about the Underground Railroad.

Back in the hotel, I took a shower, got dressed for my big night out and walked to the concert. The streets were crowded—this was a major event for the town. I'd managed to get a great seat, about ten rows back. On my left was a couple in their seventies, and on my right a couple in their sixties. A video montage played, showing clips of Barry on the piano from programs like *The Merv Griffin Show*, young and dressed up in shiny duds, playing "Mandy" or some other favourite. Then he walked out onstage and people freaked.

I freaked.

I knew the words to every song. He talked between songs about his charitable organization that donates instruments to schools because the arts, in a lot of places, are no more. He performed for maybe an hour and a half. I don't think I sat down once.

Then I went back to my hotel and went to bed. I had a flight to catch at seven the next morning, a birthday party to prepare for, a dad and family back home to celebrate. I would do so refreshed and fed by this brief escape into Barry's showbiz, into Ali's amazing accomplishments and—through these interludes with those inspiring role models—deeper into myself.

I'd been away for less than twenty-four hours, but boy, did those hours count.

The work–life balance question

I'm an interviewer by trade, but I'm no stranger to the other side of the microphone. When I'm the one being interviewed, usually about some aspect of my career, the number-one question is "Work–life balance—how do you do it?" I mostly get this question from women. I used to answer it in all the ways you'd expect: *I try to do the best that I can. I don't always get things done. I feel guilty about that. I wonder if I'm there for my kids enough.* Beating myself up.

Then, in 2015, *Canada AM* secured an exclusive interview with Gloria Steinem. What a privilege it was to sit down with her for half an hour and talk. She had just released a book called *My Life on the Road*, in which she talks about how she's spent so much of her career in transit, travelling—how she's never really spent a lot of time at home. Many of her trips involved giving talks on college and university campuses. As we spoke, she reflected on how those visits made her feel the future was in such good hands and how she encountered so many bright minds. But then she said something along these lines: "You know what? Young women, about to graduate and embark on their careers, would often ask me, 'How are we going to get married, have kids and do everything well?' Of the thousands of places I've visited, no young man ever asked that question. Not one. Ever."

I thought about that, about how the burden of managing everything is still so often reflexively taken on by women. We do it to ourselves. I realized I harboured not just guilt, but a quiet rage, when people would ask me the question about work–life balance. It's a cop-out. It's too easy. Please come up with something else.

Fuelled by, I have to confess, a simmering resentment, I began posing the question myself in interviews — not to women but to men. After listing all their accomplishments, I'd say something like, "I notice you have four kids. How do you do all that and balance time with your family?"

I'd often be met with long pauses. With, say, "I've never been asked that before." And, sometimes, answers that were quite thoughtful. There are men out there who want to make sure they spend time with their families and are trying to do better on that front. But even these men were at least slightly taken aback. It wasn't a question they were used to being asked.

Now, when the work–life balance question comes my way, I answer it differently. No more beating myself up. Instead, I say I've thrown balance out the window. I will not hold myself to that standard anymore. I'm not going to do it. I tell myself I'm a really good role model for the boy and girl I have. They see a mom who works hard and who cares about her work. I'm not going to feel guilty about doing something that I love. I've just stopped doing that. It was driving me crazy.

I won't be in

A utumn 2015. Election season. Busy, intense. I was in the car on my way to meet my trainer for a session, and I was livid.

I boxed in those days. My regular appointment with my trainer helped keep me on track: an appointment's a commitment I won't break. He would lead me through an intense forty-five-minute circuit that included treadmill work, pushups, weights, and boxing techniques: uppercuts, jabs, slips, even some sparring. I love boxing as a workout regimen. It's like swimming: it uses every part of your body. And it requires all of your attention. Focus is key. I found that if my mind drifted to some story we were working on, I wouldn't have the technique down. My trainer would say, "Marci, you're here now.

Pay attention." In boxing, you can get hurt if you don't stay alert. You start to slip, and then you fall.

Then, of course, you get back up—because as much as it's about focus, boxing is also about perseverance. Quite the metaphor for life.

But I didn't choose boxing for its life lessons. Those are insights you pick up later on, after practising those skills over and over, being pushed and corrected and cajoled by your trainer. At first, its attraction was way more visceral. Let's face it: punching a focus mitt is a great way to work out your frustrations. It's satisfying. Obviously, you can't punch real people and get away with it. But who's going to stop you from envisioning a face on that mitt you're about to wallop with your glove? No one will ever even know—no one but you.

It was one of those days when I truly needed that workout. As I drove toward the gym, I asked myself what else I could do. I didn't really have any choice. I would protest the only way I could: I would not go to work the following morning.

I'd better back up. In news, a federal election is about as big as it gets. It's all hands on deck. *Canada AM* had abandoned its regular programming in order to cover the lead-up to the federal election. Bev and I had adopted a town-hall-style approach, inviting each party leader onto the show for an extended interview with us, followed by questions from the studio audience. Our aim was to give our nationwide audience a good look at each leader contending for the country's top job: the chance to hear their views on a wide range of topics and how they responded to the concerns of Canadians. We'd already had Justin Trudeau, Thomas Mulcair and Elizabeth May on the show. That left just Stephen Harper.

After the show that morning, on my way to our post-mortem meeting, I ran into our Ottawa producer in the hallway. I was surprised to see her. Why would she be in Toronto in the midst of election season?

"Hi," I said. "What are you doing here?"

"I'm here for the interview."

"What interview?"

She explained to me that she was producing the interview with Stephen Harper that Bev was to conduct later that day. The interview would take place in Mississauga. All the details were in place.

Except one. Nobody had told me, the other co-host of the show.

I went to see the president of news, my boss's boss. I told her I wasn't happy. She, in turn, spoke to my boss and asked what was going on. It appeared that Harper wasn't willing to adhere to our format. They'd invited him to come to the studio; he'd declined. My boss and producers felt that if we insisted, we wouldn't get an interview with him at all. He was the prime minister; it was election time. So they negotiated this sit-down with Bev.

But how did this solution, hatched privately without my knowledge or input, make us look like a team? Why were we bending to his wishes? Offering him a different treatment, a different kind of platform, than we'd given all the other leaders? It smacked of favouritism.

I felt disrespected, as though my opinion didn't matter. But at my session with my trainer, I kept my focus: I punched, and I punched hard. Harder than normal. He asked what was wrong. I told him, "Work stuff."

After boxing, I called my control room producer and told her I was sick and wouldn't be in the next morning. She knew I was upset, and she knew why. She said, "Are you sure?" I said, "Absolutely. I'm not coming in." I would not sit at the desk, on the air, beside Bev, while that interview with Harper played back. I hung up, spent the evening with my family as usual, went to bed and slept.

What I had done was extreme. You don't call in sick for a national morning show during election season. You come to work. I knew there was a chance I'd be seriously reprimanded. Maybe fired. But I'd made up my mind: this was the sword I'd die on. I felt that strongly.

In the morning, the phone rang. Nanci MacLean, a vice-president at Bell Media who had recently become the lead executive on *Canada AM*, wanted to speak with me. Her assistant was calling to ask for a convenient time. I set a time. Then I said to Lloyd, "I think I'm in serious trouble."

When the call came in, though, I was shocked. It was about something else entirely. Thanksgiving weekend was coming up, and one of the co-hosts of *The Social*, CTV's daytime talk show, was going to be away for an extra day. Nanci wanted to know if I'd guest co-host. I happily accepted. But first I asked her, "Why me?"

And she replied, "Because I want to see you outside the box you're in."

I liked the sound of that. At that moment in my life, I liked it a lot.

On cloud Stevie

S ome weeks, the surprises just don't stop.

   That same week—the week I stayed home to protest the interview with Harper; the week I received that call from Nanci asking me to fill in on *The Social*; the week she chose to release me, briefly, from "the box I was in"—a *Canada AM* producer received a call from one of Stevie Wonder's people. Stevie was looking for me. Was I available? Could I get to the Air Canada Centre that evening? Would I get up onstage with him? And sing?

   Um, say what?

So here's the thing. Stevie was indeed performing that night, a show he'd said would be his final performance. Knowing that,

I'd bought tickets. And in anticipation of the event, we'd had him on the show. I'd interviewed him via satellite a couple of weeks before.

It was one of those rich, wide-ranging, in-depth interviews. We covered a lot of ground. His childhood. His early days in Motown. His longevity in the business. Politics—how some artists don't want to get involved, while his career had been defined in large part by the way he'd stood up for certain things. In 1985, he'd released an album that contained a protest song called "It's Wrong (Apartheid)." He'd been arrested at an anti-apartheid protest outside the South African Embassy in Washington, DC. And he'd accepted his Oscar for his song "I Just Called to Say I Love You," from the soundtrack for the film *The Woman in Red*, in honour of Nelson Mandela, who was then imprisoned on charges of planning to overthrow the South African government. After that, Stevie Wonder's music was actually banned by the South African regime, which controlled all broadcasting media in the country. We spoke about how he'd been front and centre, not just singing, but teaching, throughout his career.

And of course we spoke about music. He's a performer who writes his own songs—not all of them do.

During the interview, I told him, "Everybody has a favourite Stevie Wonder song. This is mine." And I sang the first few lines of "Do I Do" from 1982. It was one of those songs my sister had introduced me to—one of her favourites that, like so many songs when I was a kid, had become *our* favourite. It was a kind of osmosis the way that worked. Because she was older, if she liked a song, I liked it. And there was a period when we listened to "Do I Do" a lot.

Stevie listened as I sang. Then he said to me, "Okay, when I come to Toronto, you gotta get up onstage and sing that song with me."

He said this live, mid-interview, on *Canada AM*. I laughed it off. I said, "No. When you come to Toronto, you need to come to the studio and sit down and have a proper interview with me. None of this satellite stuff."

Little did I know that Stevie is known for bringing people up onstage to sing with him during his shows. Little did I know he was, even in relation to such an off-the-cuff moment as this, a man of his word.

I was sitting on a piano bench beside Stevie Wonder. The bench was onstage at the Air Canada Centre, which was filled to the brim with an audience of thousands. I'd been led from my seat to the stage a few moments before. I looked around the stage, thinking, "I can't believe I'm up here." There was a string section, a vocal section. Dancers. Bass. It was a huge production. I said to myself, "This is a life moment. Just be here, be in it."

Stevie said, "Hi, Marci." Then he launched into the song "Do I Do," sang a few lines, stopped, and said, "Your turn."

I took a breath and did as I was told. I sang. I sang into the microphone in front of us, which was attached to Stevie's piano. I'd sung at school events and at Ryerson. I'd sung on *Circle Square*, and in the recording studios for our albums. I'd sung at church. But this was a level of singing in public leagues beyond anything I'd ever done. I tried to forget where I was and sink into this song I'd loved since childhood, one that my sister and I had sung and danced to around the house. I called up the strong singing voice that, deep down, I knew I had. I sang up a storm.

Unbeknownst to me, my good friend Dwight Drummond, still back at our seats, was recording me on his phone. He shot the scene as if he was recording a major news event, applying his formidable camera skills to the shoot. (He'd gotten his start in the business as a camera operator with City TV.)

I'd come downtown after work and met Dwight on the way after he was finished reading the news at CBC's main studio. Earlier, waiting for the concert to start, I was in full-on, stage-fright, heart-attack mode. I said to Dwight, "I can't do this." He said, "Yes, you can." I said, "What was I thinking? This is a huge mistake." He shook his head. I whispered to him, "I'm quietly dying. I'm quietly dying."

He had to push me out of my seat. "Just go!"

After the song was over, I danced for a moment with one of the dancers onstage. And then someone led me back to join Dwight.

As soon as I sat down, my phone started to blow up. "Was that you onstage?" "Girl!! You can sing!" My sister's phone, too. Lloyd was away on business, out of town—his phone went crazy, too. My new boss, Nanci, the woman who had just recruited me to fill in on *The Social*, got a text from her assistant, who was at the concert. She'd taken a picture of me up there, sent it, and asked, "Isn't this the woman who was in your office a couple of days ago?" Nanci sent me a text right away: "Is this you with Stevie?"

In the morning, I was interviewed by colleagues at CTV, still caught up in how surreal it all was—I was still on, as I put it to them, "cloud Stevie." I remember saying, "This isn't the sort of thing you put on a bucket list because you would never in a million years think it's possible." I'd sat on a piano bench beside Stevie Wonder and sung with him. Who expects such a moment in their life?

A few days later I was on *The Social*, being peppered excitedly by the show's other three hosts, talking about sharing a stage and microphone with the legendary Stevie Wonder. Little did I know this wild week, with that incredible surprise at its core, would mark a huge turning point in my career.

"Goodbye, Canada"

The news crawl on CBC Newsworld, our competitor, the *other* national twenty-four-hour news channel, read, in bright yellow lettering, "After 43 years, *Canada AM* comes to an end. Last show tomorrow."

Instead of breaking the news, we had *become* the breaking news. It was summer 2016, and *Canada AM*, the CTV show for which I'd worked for 15 years, as a news anchor and then as co-host, was being cancelled. A new morning show would be launched by the network and none of the co-hosts would be part of it.

There had been rumours that something was coming. For a long time, we didn't know what. Finally, on a Thursday after the show, we were all called to a meeting with Nanci, who announced that the show was no more. There was a collective gasp from the team. I held the hand of one of our producers, Kristen Rynax. She and I would go on to produce a Bell Let's Talk special together. But we didn't know that then. People were afraid for their jobs until Nanci explained that most of the crew would shift over to the new morning show. Others would begin in new roles at the network. Behind the scenes, then, the same team would be working together. What would change was what viewers would see. The mix of content. The format. And, of course, us: the hosts.

The next morning, Friday, would be our last show. We got into gear and did what we'd all done together for years: we planned it, segment by segment, guest by guest, down to the final second.

Doing that show was excruciating. Our guests included contributors and experts who'd been weekly fixtures on *Canada AM* for years, including medical contributor Dr. Marla Shapiro and film critic Richard Crouse. We reminisced about memorable stories, pieces and events that had marked us or stood out in the history of the show. Seamus, who'd sat in the co-host chair for a decade, had heard the show was cancelled when it became a headline the previous afternoon. He hopped on a train and walked in halfway through the show. He wanted to be there.

We all did our best to be professional, but we were just holding it together. It felt like a funeral. I ducked under the desk during commercial breaks, trying to hide my tears from everyone who had gathered in the studio.

Each host said a few words of farewell. Jeff, who was already planning to retire later that year and move to Prince Edward

Island, spoke about what a privilege it had been. Bev said *Canada AM* had been the greatest job of her life. I talked about being a kid from Scarborough getting a chance to make history, to be part of this incredible team.

Then it was time to sign off. For good. I knew the moment had arrived. The last words fell to me. I hesitated.

News anchors and hosts often have signature sign-offs. The most famous of these include mid-twentieth-century American journalist Edward R. Murrow's "Good night, and good luck" and *CBS Evening News* anchor Walter Cronkite's "And that's the way it is." CBC's Knowlton Nash said two simple words — "Good night" — to Canadians for a decade at the end of *The National*, a sign-off his successor Peter Mansbridge once described as a "lullaby for Canadians." At CTV, Lloyd Robertson would close the evening news with these words: "That's the kind of day it's been."

At *Canada AM*, every morning for five years, I'd ended the show with a simple and cheerful "Goodbye, Canada."

The clock was running down. Our floor director was gesturing. Bev said, "OK, Marci, this is it. Say what you normally say."

I heard the floor director counting: four, three . . . I opened my mouth. I squeaked it out, through tears, with not a millisecond to spare.

"Goodbye, Canada."

And we went to black.

Last day of *Canada AM*. (*From left*: Seamus O'Regan, me, Bev Thomson and Jeff Hutcheson.)

Embrace this change

The place was called Catcha Falling Star, a getaway nestled in the oceanside cliffs of Negril, a small Jamaican vacation town that's known for its seven-mile beach and its Coral Reef Preservation Society.

According to the *New York Times* Negril was the setting for a 1965 novel by Ian Fleming called *The Man with the Golden Gun*. But I wasn't in Negril for intrigue. I'd organized a week of childcare shared by my husband, my sister and some friends and I hightailed it to Jamaica, my comfort place—as I always do, if at all possible, when I need to regroup, recharge and recollect myself.

A serious amount of all three was very much in order. *Canada AM* was no more, and I was devastated. It takes time and introspection to understand that change, when thrust upon you, can be an opportunity.

Some people, my husband included, recommended I march into my boss's office and demand to know why I wasn't part of this new show to be launched, which was called *Your Morning* and was to be hosted by Ben Mulroney and Anne-Marie Mediwake. But the truth was that I didn't want to be part of it. I was done with the early hours. I was done with getting up at two thirty in the morning. I didn't have it in me anymore.

Still. It was a mammoth shift, and I had no idea where it might lead. I'd begun filling in as a guest co-host on *The Social*, but I had no sense of what my next move might be or what opportunities I should pursue. My new boss said, "You've got some time. You may never get this chunk of time again. Take it." I decided she was right. When would I get another chance? It felt so urgent—to get away, take time, think, reassess—that I missed my long-time friend and colleague Jeff Hutcheson's retirement party. I said to him, "You know how much I love you, but I've got to get out of here." And I did. I left town.

The place in Negril was small, beautiful, perfect. I had no schedule, no plan. I stayed in a small tiki hut and spent time in the sun, writing, my surroundings awash in gorgeous flowers and fruit-bearing trees. I ate delicious local food. I kept a journal of my thoughts, some of them personal and others about what might come next professionally. In it were ideas for shows I might want to pitch. Chief among these was a show called *Transition*, and it would be about people navigating some major life change, whether by choice or circumstance. Obviously, transitions were top of mind for me. But I believed it was a winning premise for a show. I'd still like to pursue it someday. The most interesting time in a person's life is when they're faced with change, whether they're a lifelong cab driver thrown off course by the rise of Uber, someone newly married or newly divorced, someone undergoing a sex change, or someone in jail coming back into the community to make a fresh start. Do they swim? Do they sink? How do they forge a new path? What happens?

Three things happened during the week I spent in Negril. First, Muhammad Ali died. His funeral, which was shown live on CNN, was the only thing I watched on television that week. The cameras followed the funeral procession through the streets of Louisville all the way to the stadium, the same place I'd seen Barry Manilow perform the previous summer. I recognized the streetscape and landmarks along the route, including the Muhammad Ali Center. As I'd felt while making my way through that museum and its exhibits advocating non-violent change, watching the funeral, I was overcome with a sense of possibility and hope. A Jewish rabbi got up and spoke about Ali. Orrin Hatch, a white senator from the South, explained to everyone how and why he and this Muslim Black man, way back in the civil rights era, had become friends. All these people from all these walks of life memorializing this great man in front of the millions watching: this was how the world should look.

Second, I thought long and hard about the life I'd been living, the pace of it, how just keeping that up took every ounce of energy I had. I knew—I'd already decided, but as the week progressed I became more and more certain it was the right call—that I wasn't going to walk into my boss's office and ask why I wasn't on the new morning show. The hours of solitude solidified in my heart that I was doing the right thing. It was time to redirect and reclaim myself. My days of doing breaking news were probably over. I wanted to explore other things. I gave myself permission to do that. It was time to use my voice in a different way.

Third, I was contacted by the producer of a speaker series in Toronto called Women of Influence, which aims to foster female empowerment in part through sharing the stories of role models. They run a speaker series at Roy Thomson Hall featuring successful women from all over the world: politicians, authors, entrepreneurs. Their series host had cancelled at the last minute. They found me on the beach somehow and emailed to ask if I could step in and interview American neuroscientist and author Lisa Genova. Her novel *Still Alice*, about a professor suffering early on-set Alzheimer's, had become an Oscar-winning film starring Julianne Moore. The event was the following Tuesday; I was to fly home Sunday. I thought, *OK. This is what I do. Time to get back in the saddle.* So I said yes.

The interview felt, to me, profound. Genova's story was inspiring. She was a Harvard-trained scientist with a successful career and a young child; she just knew that she had a book in her. So she'd walked away from her job. She spoke about leaving her child in daycare and sitting in a coffee shop writing all day and everyone around her telling her she was crazy. Her area of scientific expertise was memory, so in her fiction, she dove deep into Alzheimer's and its impacts on people and their families. But when she was finished, she couldn't find an agent or publisher to take the book. Instead of giving up and putting the manuscript away, she self-published it. Beverly Beckham, a writer for the *Boston Globe*, read the book and raved about it in a piece. Beckham wrote that the literary agents who'd said *Still Alice* wouldn't sell, that it would only interest people in the Alzheimer's "community," were wrong, that when she'd finished the slim book, she wanted to "stand up and tell a train full of strangers" they had to read it. That was when things began to change for Genova and her new career as an author.

She'd walked away from her life. She'd manufactured her own transition. She'd taken her scientific knowledge and made from it a piece of art—one that opened millions of minds and hearts to the heartache and challenge of neurological disease. My own transition wasn't one I'd gone looking for, but it had come my way. I decided to embrace it.

A new chapter

My dad sometimes said to me in the months after *Canada AM* was cancelled, "What if this was all for you? What if this show ended for you, Marci?"

I knew what he meant. It was his way of saying change, even when you didn't go looking for it, can be wrapped in opportunity. "What if this happened," Dad said, "so you could understand what's possible?"

Sure enough, of the three former hosts, Bev, Jeff and me, it was my life that took the most dramatic turn. Bev stayed in news, while Jeff's retirement and move to PEI had already been set. Me, I left the people I knew and had worked with for fifteen years, left the very building I'd worked in since my late twenties, my professional comfort zone.

It happened like this. One of the regular co-hosts of *The*

Social, Traci Melchor, was away on extended leave. For a month or so, I served as a guest co-host, rotating with other guests. On top of appearing on *The Social*, I continued to work on possible pitches for new initiatives, such as the idea for the show *Transition* I'd come up with in Jamaica. And the Women of Influence event I'd guest hosted upon my return from Jamaica became a permanent gig that I would hang on to for the next two years. Some months later, when it became clear that the seat on *The Social* I was filling daily as a guest co-host was going to be available for good, I was hired to fill it. I had officially moved downtown to CTV's production studios.

Not everyone in my life was happy about this change. My mom wasn't keen on the sometimes racy subject matter. Lloyd felt I was dropping a notch career-wise in moving from serious journalism to what he termed a "gossip" show. But I begged— and still beg—to differ.

The Social is a lively, viewer-focused talk show on which I, with my co-hosts Melissa Grelo, Cynthia Loyst, Lainey Lui and Jess Allen, energetically mull the latest news, current affairs and cultural and lifestyle issues. Our audience stands cheering as we walk, on-air, into the studio each afternoon. We incorporate comments from viewers through Facebook, Instagram, Twitter and other social media formats into our discussions, in real time, on the air. People have called the show a "well-oiled machine," but the fact is, the machine doesn't run without a talented crew, dedicated producers and our executive team.

On a given day, we'll share, discuss and even outright debate our opinions on topics ranging from the personal tale of a survivor of human trafficking; Whitney Houston's Hologram Tour and the ethical questions that raises; whether it's tough to be managed by a boss who's much younger than you are; the quality of gay marriages versus straight marriages (this discussion was based on a study that suggested gay marriages are often happier); and the question of whether it's bad form to lean your seat back on an airplane (this lighthearted, controversial topic came up one day in the weeks preceding the COVID-19 pandemic, when people's travel-related concerns were so much less fraught than they were soon, so suddenly, to become). We'll touch on celebrities: Drake, Kanye West, Taylor Swift, Beyoncé. We've interviewed cultural icons, pop stars and political leaders ranging from Sting, Ice Cube, Ryan Reynolds and Emma Thompson to Prime Minister Justin Trudeau and other politicians, as well as sports figures, authors, and health and lifestyle experts. Other guests who sat on our grey couch to chat include — to offer a very small sample — journalist Tanya Talaga on the state of reconciliation in Canada; Robyn Doolittle, who was on the show to talk about her book *Had It Coming*, which delved into the sexual politics of the #MeToo movement; and Desmond Cole (who famously walked away from a journalism career to become an activist) on the state of anti-Black racism in Canada. When COVID-19 was declared a pandemic, we rebooted the show to broadcast from our living rooms, tackling timely topics such as how to strike a balance between home schooling and work, maintaining mental health, dispelling myths about the virus, how to disinfect items in your home, how to properly practise social distancing, and whether you should order takeout food (and all the issues that raises, from a duty to support small or local businesses to the risks posed to delivery workers).

The women who host this show, and the folks who produce it, are smart, accomplished people. I find *The Social* freeing after so many years working as a straight-up journalist. I no longer need to distance myself from the news: I'm not duty bound to be impartial. On the contrary. My opinion—my still very well-informed opinion—is called for. It's requested. If I'm touched or moved by something happening in the news, it's not only OK to show that, it's my job. Bottom line: I get to speak my mind.

Lifestyle and entertainment programming is nothing like news. When I was first working on *The Social*, I felt out of my element. It wasn't my house. I was a visitor. How much do I speak? Before it was telling stories about other people, now it's about telling mine. What are we hoping to achieve? Where do we put our energies, our emphasis? But I soon found my footing and realized that I was able to enrich the show with my perspective and with my journalism background: we could get newsier with our topics while still keeping our opinions. I also brought in a new stream of viewers. Many people in their forties, fifties and sixties who'd watched me for years on *Canada AM* turned to *The Social* out of curiosity. In some ways, because I have a voice on this show, my own personal voice, I feel more than ever like I can act as a voice for the communities I come from and connect with, in particular the Black community. And I have to say, my move from a national morning news show to a daily talk show has not dissuaded the Prime Minister's Office from calling. Most recently, they reached out in February 2020 to ask me to interview Justin Trudeau at a Black History Month event at the National Arts Centre in Ottawa.

Canada AM, though, remains a cornerstone of my life and my career. And its impact lingers in ways that both surprise me and don't. In 2018, two years after the show's cancellation, I was named one of Canada's Most Powerful Women by the Women's Executive Network. The following year, when my co-host Melissa Grelo was one of the honourees, I was asked to host the annual awards gala. During a break in the evening, General Jon Vance, who was serving as chief of defence staff of the Canadian Armed Forces, approached me and introduced himself.

"Hi, General Vance," I said. "Yes, I know you—we did several interviews together on *Canada* AM." They'd been conducted via satellite, so I added, "It's nice to see you in person."

Then I realized he wasn't just being friendly; he had something to tell me. He said, "I want you to know that when we were in Afghanistan, we watched your newscast in the morning. For two years you were with us. Watching you was like having a little bit of home with us."

I asked if I could hug him.

"Of course," he replied.

I gave him a huge hug.

Then he said, "I want you to have this. It's a special coin I give to special people." And he handed me a gold coin the size of a silver dollar. It had red stones in it and his name engraved along the perimeter. My eyes welled with tears.

That experience was singular, but it wasn't unfamiliar. As I write this, it's been four years since *Canada* AM's chapter in

Canadian broadcasting closed. Yet not a single day passes (no exaggeration, I truly mean not one single day) when I don't encounter a person—on the subway, in *The Social*'s studio audience, over Twitter—who says something like, "We miss you so much on *Canada AM*."

In this business, you never know who's watching. You never know if you're making a difference. I'm fortunate that once in a while, powerful proof comes along to say, "Yes. Yes, you are."

Passing the torch. Traci leaves *The Social*, and I officially join the show. (*From left*: Melissa Grelo, me, Traci Melchor, Lainey Lui and Cynthia Loyst.)

The bathtub talk

W e were backstage at *The Social*. I'd had my makeup done. We sat where we gather before going on-air — around the big table there with our laptops, notebooks, pens, pencils. It was minutes before showtime. We were having our last meeting about that day's topics.

Usually we're four or five around the table: me, Melissa Grelo, Cynthia Loyst, Lainey Lui and Jess Allen. With us that morning was a guest co-host, one of our regulars, the woman we refer to as our Sixth *Social* Sister: singer, songwriter, actress, author and Order of Canada recipient Jann Arden. That somewhat daunting resumé belies the intuitive warmth of this woman who, in those moments before the show, saw something in my face, took my hand, fixed her eyes on mine and asked me how I was.

When Jann looks at you, she's looking directly at you—no, *through* you, picking up every nuance. It's this seeing-into-your-soul kind of look.

I told her I was fine. We both knew that wasn't true.

When I got home that evening, it was a bit late, as I'd attended an event. It had been the annual gala for the Pinball Clemons Foundation, a charity co-founded by family friends Mike Clemons and Diane Lee Clemons (who's also my business partner in our accessories company, IEN LEE—more on that later), and I was dressed up in a black satin pantsuit and heels. Lloyd was working downstairs. I went straight up to our room, walked into the bathroom, sat on the edge of the tub and called Jann. She answered right away.

"Hi," I said. "What did you see in me that worried you today?"

"Your eyes. They look sad. They've lost that spark," she said.

You can't hide things from your friends. It doesn't matter whether you're trying to shield them from worrying about your worries—or shielding yourself from having to face up to those worries. Your friends see it. They know.

The fact is, I felt lonely. I remembered my sister saying this a long time ago, before her marriage ended—I think she must have felt the same way. I wasn't lonely before I got married. It's ironic: I literally had to get married to feel this way. Because when you're married, you're supposed to have a partner, someone who's beside you, who's supportive, who's working with you on this thing we call a shared life.

I, however, felt immense loneliness. Like there really was no "us." I felt I was on my own, abandoned in many ways.

Lloyd and I would talk about it. He would say our jobs are very busy, we both travel a lot. We have to do better.

But I knew many busy couples, people who were every bit as busy as we were, who had good relationships. Who were happily married. I could tell the difference. I was coming around to accepting that something was wrong at the core of this marriage—and that something needed to be done.

What had happened? Lloyd and I had been married for seventeen years. We'd made a family: Blaize was thirteen and Dash, six. We ran a smooth household. We weren't nasty to one another. Daily life wasn't obviously terrible. But there was a hole in the middle of it.

I made plans alone, went on trips—like that fast getaway to see Barry Manilow—alone. It wasn't that there were constant disagreements or arguments. Nor was it that we were our own people, doing our own things—you have to be your own person to be part of a healthy couple. There was this sense of being apart, separate, not united, that never seemed to change, that went all the way back to how I'd felt that night not long after the car accident, when Lloyd got dressed and went into work. A sense of caring and love underlines a strong marriage; even when it's not being openly shown or expressed, you feel it. You know that person is beside you, even when they're annoyed with you. Even after a heated argument, you feel it: you have both given yourselves to this union, and even in rough patches, you're scrambling for footholds and new pathways together.

I had been waiting for a long time to find this sense of togetherness. Why was I just coming to recognize this now—or rather, to finally accept that things inside this marriage weren't going to get better? It might have been that I was simply done with waiting. And I guess part of the answer is that you get to a place when you're ready to get there. For so many years I'd worked the morning news shift, getting up every weekday at three: I was so busy trying to survive, I was on autopilot. I put my clothes out the night before, put my children's clothes out the night before. Made sure homework was done, lunches were made and my notes were ready. I read the books I needed to read. I did all I had to do, and then I went to sleep, got up, went to work and did it all again. When *Canada AM* was cancelled in 2016, that punishing schedule stopped, just like that. There were several months of uncertainty and exploration, and then came *The Social*. Working on this show felt different; there was space, a little more time. The way I was living my life, the way my marriage functioned—and didn't function—ever so gradually began to sink in.

Meanwhile, I was turning fifty. At this point you can't deny having reached and moved well into—or beyond—middle age. All at once, time becomes a precious commodity. If things aren't getting better, are you going to just keep waiting for that to happen? Are you willing to give up more of your time? Are you prepared to stay unhappy?

· · ·

Jann and I spoke for an hour that night as I sat on the edge of the tub in my fancy clothes, cradling the phone. I told her, "Things aren't going well with Lloyd. It's been hard."

She said, "Marci, do whatever you have to do to make yourself whole. To get that happiness back. There is so much light on the other side."

Jann wasn't the only friend who'd checked in, expressed concern, spoken up. Another friend had said to me, "You've lived the first half of your life this way. Are you going to continue for the second half, or are you going to change it up?"

My sister had said, "You're still young. This is not throwing-in-the-towel time. Either you are fine living this way, or you change it."

I opted to change it. I drew courage from the words of my sister—have I mentioned that on top of everything else she's taught me, my sister is the one who has shown me when it's time to take a risk? I drew courage from the words of my friends. From that bathtub conversation with Jann. From my own inner resolve. Finally, I said to Lloyd, "It isn't our fault. We didn't know how to do this. We never saw, growing up, a relationship that worked." My parents had divorced, and Lloyd's father had died when he was young. I told him, "I want our kids to know what love looks like. I don't want them to grow up seeing dysfunction. If they see an example, I want them to see a loving one."

Also, I wanted to survive. To regain my wholeness. To remember who I was, free of that cloud of loneliness. If a friend had come to me with issues like mine, my advice would absolutely have been the same: Live your life. Don't settle. I see too many people selling themselves, and their happiness, short. I know that no one's ever truly *completely* happy, but I do believe that a state resembling happiness exists and that we can and should reach toward it.

It would be another year before Lloyd and I would separate.

Jann Arden and me backstage at Roy Thomson Hall. I interviewed Jann for a Unique Lives & Experiences event.

The kids from Dene

I had been calling Dene High School in La Loche, Saskatchewan, repeatedly for over a week, leaving messages for the school principal, Greg Hatch.

Later, I would learn that Greg was the school's former principal and athletics coach and had been en route to retirement when he was asked to come back. The bulk of the school's administration team had taken mental health leave after a shooting at the school several months earlier. Greg had stepped up and returned as acting principal. At this point, though, all I knew was that I was being told he wasn't available to take my call. So I'd leave a message and call back the next day. Then I'd leave another message. And so on.

Finally, one day, after identifying myself as I always did—as

Marci Ien from CTV—I made it absolutely clear that I wasn't calling in a news capacity.

That day, Greg took the call.

I'd been all set to leave yet another message—it was becoming a habit—and suddenly there he was, on the line. Thus began a series of events I could never have foreseen.

Greg now says my call that day was the best call he ever took.

Several months before, on Friday, January 22, 2016, in the village of La Loche, Saskatchewan, a nightmare unfolded. A seventeen-year-old boy killed two brothers in their home over their school lunch break and then made his way back to Dene High School, where he'd attended classes that morning. Once there, he shot and killed a teacher and a teacher's aide and injured seven others. The shooting spree was said to be a reaction to the boy not being well liked at school. The tragedy was a top story across the country, and we covered it extensively on *Canada AM* in the days that followed. We had news hits each hour with our reporters on the ground and carried live press conferences held by everyone from the RCMP to the mayor of the community of three thousand to the premier of Saskatchewan to the prime minister.

The story stirred my soul in a big way. It was the people who broke my heart. The students and staff who lost family and friends. Those who were seriously injured and the many whose injuries weren't apparent because mental anguish and trauma aren't usually visible. As a reporter asking questions, though, you recognize the signs. In people's body language. In their eyes. In their responses. It's not necessarily what's said but what isn't.

As a reporter, I was no stranger to devastating stories. It was often my duty to report on tragic events. But this one hit me hard because the setting was close to home. These were teachers and students. I'm the daughter of an educator. I had come so close to taking that career path myself, to becoming a teacher. I had a niece in high school and a daughter on the verge.

I couldn't sleep.

What's more, the event had taken place in a small and remote First Nations community. That also hit home for me. I'd always had a keen interest in issues facing Indigenous Peoples and wanted to amplify these topics more than we sometimes did on our program and in our news department.

When the shooting happened in La Loche, these things came together: schools and the struggles Indigenous Peoples face on a daily basis. With that story, everything that might trigger me did. I thought the situation there, in that tiny community, is in some ways already going to be desperate. I dug deeper and learned that the suicide rate in La Loche was the highest in the province and three times the national average. It was literally one tragedy after another, and now this had happened. A perfect storm of sadness.

I went home one afternoon when La Loche was still very much in the news and picked up the paper. The *Globe and Mail*. I stared at it. A picture jumped out at me that I obviously hadn't noticed that morning. Students were seated in a circle around what looked like a campfire. The article explained that these young people were participating in a forgiveness circle: in Dene culture, if someone does something wrong, everyone—the whole community—is responsible. So the community as a whole was seeking forgiveness. I thought that was extraordinary. That in this time of pain, the community was pivoting to forgiveness.

I noticed that one of the kids in the photograph was wearing a Toronto Raptors cap. I immediately wondered if anyone at head office had seen it. What if the team could do something to help this community that had suffered so much? I had interviewed the team's president, Masai Ujiri, a couple of times through the years. I knew that he ran a basketball program for kids in Africa during the summer and thought he might be willing to help the kids at Dene High.

I didn't have his phone number and was reluctant to call the newsroom and ask for it, as the story was still active and I was going way beyond the call of duty. Journalists aren't meant to get involved in the stories they report on: they're supposed to maintain distance and neutrality. But I was compelled, too moved by what had happened in La Loche, to not follow this impulse. I decided to try a variety of email addresses ending in "raptors.com." I simply put "school shooting" in the subject line, typed in my cellphone number and asked Masai if he could spare a few minutes to talk. One of the addresses worked. My phone began to ring. I answered it.

"Marci? It's Masai. How can I help?"

I was shocked he was on the other end of the line. Just like that. And I heard kindness in his voice.

"Masai. Thanks for calling. Have you seen the front of the

Globe and Mail today? The kids from Dene High School in La Loche, where that shooting took place, held what's called a forgiveness circle. One of them is wearing your team cap. I thought maybe there's something that can be done for the community—for the kids."

"Can you send me a screen shot?"

"Sure."

He received it and said, "Leave it with me. I'll see what we can do."

I thanked him and hung up.

Six months later, I was guest co-hosting *The Social* one day when Masai was scheduled to join us. *Giants of Africa*, the documentary about his non-profit foundation that runs basketball camps for youth in several African countries, had been nominated for a Canadian Screen Award. Masai spoke about the film and about the program he'd initiated, which uses basketball as a tool for education and that has enriched the lives of hundreds of youth.

After his segment, Masai pulled me aside. He told me he hadn't forgotten about the kids in La Loche. He said he thought that sometimes it was better to act *after* the cameras had gone and the headlines were long past—that this was when support was most needed. I agreed.

The timing was good for other reasons as well. I was no longer part of a news team. My role as guest co-host of *The Social* fell outside the bounds of journalism within which I'd operated for so many years. I was free to get more involved. To advocate. Speak up. Try to help.

A week later, Masai and I met in his office to strategize. We got right down to business. What can we do? What might be useful? Money? Clothes? Shoes? Boots? Masai has relationships with athletic-wear companies. We put together a list of things we thought we could collect and donate from afar. I thought we needed to phone the school and ask what they needed so we could narrow it down.

That brought me to my series of calls to Greg—calls he wasn't taking. I now know that he heard the words "Marci" and "CTV" and thought about how every part of the news media had already been to Dene High and covered the story. How the news media had descended on Dene High after the shooting when it was a hot story—and then disappeared. The school community was hurting and he just didn't want to deal with more unwanted attention.

But then one day, someone working in the office said to him, "This Marci woman's on the phone again." She told him I'd made it abundantly clear I wasn't calling in a news capacity. And he got on the line.

Greg comes from Dryden, Ontario. He was an outstanding hockey player who studied on scholarship in the United States. He decided he wanted to teach, but when he finished his education degree, there weren't a lot of jobs available. One came up in this little town in northern Saskatchewan. He was young and thought, "What do I have to lose?" He took the job and moved north in 1976 and ended up spending his life there. In 1983, he coached the Dene basketball team to a provincial championship. He learned to speak Dene. He met and married the love of his life, Albertine, a woman from the local Dene community; they have kids and grandkids. The gymnasium at the school is named after him. He is well loved in the community, a real father figure.

I would learn all that later, though. I was just grateful to have Greg on the phone at last. I told him I'd been reporting the day the shooting happened and that I'd seen a picture of the kids in the paper and had reached out to Masai—that now the two of us wanted to know what the school needed.

"I figured I'd call," I said, "before we started just sending things there."

Greg explained that he had started a breakfast program to help keep the community together during those dark days: he thought it would help to start the day eating together. They'd opened up the kitchen and an area in the school and welcomed students and anyone else from the community from six thirty in the morning onward. He was talking about extending it to lunch, a substantial meal to keep the kids at school. He said some would go home for lunch and not come back afterward. But money was short. I began making mental notes: this meal program would need support.

Then Greg said something that changed the whole trajectory. He said, "You know what, Marci? If you really want to help, you need to see what we're about. You should come here and see us. See who we are. How we live."

I paused. I was silent, taking that in. I thought, *OK. He's got a point.* He really does. Masai and I had immediately jumped into work mode. We hadn't for a second thought about going to La Loche ourselves. I said to Greg, "I understand. You're right."

Later that day I spoke with Masai. "Listen," I said, "I finally got the principal on the phone. He's heavily suggesting we make the trip and visit Dene High School." I explained that Greg didn't want us to send things. He wanted us to see and talk to the kids, listen to their experiences, and meet him and the staff. I continued, "I do think he's right."

After a moment's thought, Masai said, "Let's look at our schedules, Marci, and find a way to get this done."

Saying it was a busy fall for me is an understatement. We had two network specials to record: a playful "gossip special," on which my co-hosts and I review the big entertainment stories of the year, and a holiday special with Jann Arden as guest. We had live studio audiences and shot each of them on a Saturday, which meant a six-day work week. I was also co-hosting the Santa Claus Parade. The Grey Cup was in Toronto that year and my co-hosts and I had been invited to host the pre-game show. My only day off over several weeks was the Monday after the Grey Cup. November 28.

That morning, Masai, Mark Vallena, a producer at Maple Leaf Sports and Entertainment, the parent company of the Raptors, and I boarded a flight from Toronto to Fort McMurray, Alberta, which is just over the provincial border from La Loche. Masai's schedule was, if anything, tighter than mine. We were doing this, but it had to be a one-day trip: fly in, visit, return that night. An optimistic—or should I say completely insane?—travel plan in a country this size with its unpredictable weather. Late

November in the northern regions of western Canada is basically full-on winter. We knew this—and yet we went.

The cloud cover in Fort McMurray that day was intense as our first flight landed. It was hard to see anything at all. I looked at Masai and knew exactly what he was thinking: Had we come this far not to get to our destination? This had to work. Somehow it did.

We boarded a small craft—the only type, apparently, that could manoeuvre in such conditions. We were lucky; many other flights had been cancelled. Though I can't say I felt exactly lucky in the moment. I honestly prayed the entire time we were in the air. We saw nothing but clouds. I was thinking, *This could be it. I don't know that we're making it.*

Then, the next thing we knew, we were landing. Greg, Martha Morin, his administrative assistant, and the school's vice-principal, Donna Janvier, were on the landing strip to greet us. We exchanged handshakes and hugs and piled into their cars to head to the school. Our pilots came with us; they were worried that if they flew back to Fort McMurray, conditions might not allow them to return and pick us up that evening.

At the school, we went to the office, put down our things, and then did a series of classroom visits, saying hello to the kids, talking with them about what they were working on. Except for a few students, they were very quiet. For the most part, they simply stared at us. Signs of the tragedy were everywhere. The shooter had torn through the building. The office, where a teacher's aide had died, was damaged. The staff room, too. There were visible bullet holes in the front door of the building, which shocked me. I doubted whether the holes would still be there

202 • Marci Ien

months after such an incident if the school were in Vancouver or Toronto. That students were still faced with these reminders on a daily basis seemed to me damning evidence of how little the outside world cared about what had happened here.

We had lunch with the staff. Conversation was, in part, about the upcoming anniversary of the shooting, which was less than two months away. Greg was talking about not wanting that kind of press and wondering how to handle it. I told him, "It's your school; you handle it the way you see fit. You can put out a press release beforehand that says you won't be speaking publicly, that the community wishes to observe a quiet time. You can do that." I said, "The important thing is to control your story. If you send something out in advance, that will help."

At the end of the day, an assembly was held. Masai told his story—about growing up in Nigeria—to the kids. How he had dreams that were bigger than the place he was in. He encouraged the kids at Dene High to do the same. Dream big. Be proud of your community and your family. But your world is bigger than La Loche. You can also dream outside of these walls—the invisible walls you may have built for yourself.

After flying back to Fort MacMurray, Masai, Mark and I shared a meal. Masai shared some thoughts. "I want to bring some kids to Toronto," he said. "It's important that they're exposed to things outside their community."

"I love the idea," I said.

Our red-eye landed in Toronto the following morning. We said our goodbyes. But we had a plan. I contacted the folks at Dene High, who were all for it: they knew this would be an opportunity for their students. I found some dates in the Raptors' schedule where there were games on a Friday and a Sunday and began to formulate an itinerary.

By early December we had a program in place. I'd reached out to my alma mater, Ryerson University, to see if they would provide dorm rooms for the kids while they were in Toronto. When I contacted Ryerson's president, Mohamed Lachemi, he said the school would provide hotel rooms for the kids and their teacher-chaperones as well as a tour of the university! Imogen Coe, a biochemist and then-dean of science at Ryerson, happened to be from the same hometown as Adam Wood, the teacher who'd been shot and killed at Dene High. She had followed the story and been deeply touched by it—it hit very close to home. She offered to put together a science lab for the students. We planned to have some student athletes or First Nations students speak to them about their own experiences.

The idea was to let them see they had options in life and that getting a post-secondary education was one of them.

We left it up to Greg, Martha and Donna to choose a group of students who they thought would most benefit from the trip. They knew the kids well. We said we'd love to have kids come who've never left the province, never been on a plane before. We don't need the outstanding students. We want the kid who's on the periphery, for whom a trip like this, the chance to see something different, could do immense good.

I'd also arranged a tour of the CN Tower, a visit to Ripley's Aquarium, a special Saturday night group dinner, and of course there were two Raptors games on the agenda. Everything was set.

That is, until I began to mull over the plan. It was Boxing Day of 2016, and I was reading a book by Will Schwalbe called *Books for Living*. I was preparing to interview Will at an upcoming event at the Toronto Public Library. TPL runs an authors' series that includes onstage interviews by journalists with an audience question-and-answer period to follow. I have partnered with the library for years and look forward to these events. I got no further than Will's introduction before I stopped cold. And began to think.

Will had written about himself and his siblings, all now in their fifties, talking about where they were in life. His brother, he wrote, uses a golf analogy to describe this. He says it's not about being on the leaderboard anymore. It's about avoiding the water hazards and sand traps. He was talking about legacy—about my dad's version of the dash. Making the most of life when you've lived more days than you're likely to have left.

I thought about the kids from Dene High School and whether we were doing all we could. As a reporter, I knew that Indigenous voters had supported Justin Trudeau's bid for the prime minister's job in record numbers. Voting had shot up so dramatically that some communities and reserves had run out of ballots. I thought the prime minister should know that this community was still suffering immensely after its loss and that the kids at Dene High School felt forgotten.

I had noticed that Katie Telford, the prime minister's chief of staff, followed me on Twitter. I sent her a direct message: "Happy holidays, Katie. Might I be able to have a brief chat with you at your earliest convenience?"

She wrote back, "Sure. Why don't you email me? Have a great day." She included her email address. I composed a lengthy, detailed note and sent it off.

Silence. I didn't hear a thing. I thought maybe I'd overdone it with the email—included too much, information overload.

The holidays over, I returned to work, and the week of the Dene students' trip drew nearer. A week away from their arrival, I received an email from the director of operations in the Prime Minister's Office, asking if we could talk. On the phone he said, "What is it that you want?"

I said, "I want these kids to be able to speak to somebody." I meant someone like the minister of Indigenous affairs. Somebody who could make them feel listened to, heard.

His reply was beyond anything I would have expected. He said that, actually, the timing might work for something more.

"You know the prime minister is doing these town halls?" he asked.

"Yes," I said.

"There's one scheduled for Toronto the day the kids are there." I said, "Are you kidding?"

He wasn't. This wasn't something we could have planned, that Justin Trudeau would be in Toronto on Friday, January 13, while our students from La Loche would be here as well. He said to me, "If this were to happen, where?"

I immediately offered up the OVO Athletic Centre, where the Raptors train (it was then called the BioSteel Centre). I know what's involved in a PM visit, the security that's required. It's off the beaten path. It's a Raptors facility. Lots of room. No unions involved. I offered it up without talking to Masai. I called him afterward and said, here's what's happened, and here's what I did.

He first said, "What?" Then he paused and said, "Marci, this is amazing."

I said, "Who should they arrange things with at the facility?"

A week later, Masai and I welcomed Prime Minister Justin Trudeau into the athletic centre. We gave him a bit of a tour then led him into the team's locker room. The kids were all there. In walked the prime minister, and we shut the door. For forty-five minutes, he took questions and talked to the kids. It was amazing.

Several of the students there had parents with mental health issues or addictions. Trudeau was very open about his childhood and being the son of a mom with bipolar disorder. He talked about growing up in a house with a mother he obviously loves dearly, but that it was hard sometimes, and how it sometimes felt like parenting a parent. The kids told him about not feeling heard and feeling like the rest of the country just didn't care about them. He said, "I want you to know that we do, and we're going to try to change that." But mostly, he listened, and it was interesting because they wanted to share. They were comfortable.

Afterward, former Raptors head coach Dwane Casey came in to chat with the kids. He talked about not having shoes as a kid. He said, sure, he was in a privileged position now. How many NBA coaches are there in the world? But getting there was an uphill fight. It took hard work, perseverance and hope. You're going to fall, he told the kids. It's about getting back up. Having your eye on a prize.

They were riveted.

Then we divided the kids into Team Casey and Team Trudeau. They all left the locker room, came out on the court and played a game of basketball. The prime minister was playing basketball with these kids.

At the Raptors game the first night, the Dene High students were announced to the fans in the stadium. They were on the floor for the national anthem. The kids that year were a huge news story: every network covered their visit. I had started a GoFundMe page for the breakfast program. Lisa LaFlamme mentioned it when the story aired on CTV News that evening. The page raised thousands of dollars that went directly to the school.

The students had arrived on a Thursday and flew back home early Monday morning. By the end of their four-day trip, I noticed kids who would barely say a few words at first were having full conversations with everybody. We could see the growth just in those few days. After they'd been home for a while, Greg and Martha reported on the differences they saw: kids who'd often skipped classes were now the first ones there. Kids came in early to help out with the breakfast program. They'd changed their tune. It was almost like they had a mission. They wanted to do well in school because they knew that would help them get to university. And the kids who'd travelled to Toronto were telling others about their experiences and putting hope in their hearts as well.

• • •

Four years have passed since then. In the interim, Masai and I
went to Ottawa with Greg and Martha, armed with a document
detailing what we thought would help the school and the community, and met with the ministers for Indigenous affairs and
finance. We impressed upon them what an important part of
the community the school was: a key amenity. A meeting place,
a gym used by all. To have it out of operation was a huge problem. What had happened after the shooting, Greg would liken
to 9/11. The school was the epicentre, but everybody around
the school had benefitted: the friendship centre got money, the
medical facility got money. But the school, which had suffered
the greatest losses, didn't.

Did our meetings on Parliament Hill make a difference?
Did the prime minister's meeting with the kids? In January
2019, Trudeau visited La Loche for the re-opening of Dene
High School. He announced $2.2 million over five years for
cultural and language-based programming, on-the-land activities and mental health services for students, all to support the
broader Holistic Healing Plan the high school had developed
and begun to implement. These days, the breakfast and lunch
programs, a key part of that plan, are in full swing, and a mental
health professional is on hand several times a month. A year or
so ago, I reached out to President's Choice Children's Charity
and told them the story of how Masai and I got involved with
Dene High. They offered to donate greenhouses and sent over
staff to get them up and running on the grounds at the school.
So the kids are now growing food to sustain their community.

Meanwhile, each winter, a group of students travel from La
Loche to Toronto. This annual trip runs under the umbrella

of Masai's Giants of Africa program and gets pulled together by a small team of people tackling logistics and travel plans, including me, Masai's assistant and the staff at Dene High. The students stay in Ryerson dorms and visit the university for talks, tours and labs. They meet Indigenous student leaders. The aquarium and the CN Tower provide tours for the group each year. We have our Saturday evening "family" dinner at The Keg. And, of course, Raptors games are on the agenda.

One of the older students who came to Toronto the first year has since begun attending film school. What other effects may transpire as the years pass? I'd like to formalize this program more and establish some methods for tracing and assessing its impact. Because, after all, what is this thing we do with the kids from La Loche? We aren't changing these kids. We aren't *improving* them. We're getting to know them. We're listening to them. We're giving them the chance to be seen for who they are—away from home, in the wider world—and to know how it feels to be seen that way. We're exposing them to leaders and to people who excel in their fields, and exposing those role models as ordinary people who've struggled, often against tremendous odds. We're giving them a set of experiences that may slightly recalibrate their perspective on themselves, their community and their ideas about their future lives. Maybe, mostly, we're giving them space: the space of a few days outside their norm; a little space that may settle within their hearts and minds and gradually open and spread; a space—I hope—within which they may make new dreams and imagine new pathways to follow.

I still think back to that first year and the first group of La Loche kids who came. The day they arrived in Toronto, they were brought to the CTV studios and appeared on *The Social*. My co-hosts asked them questions, and the kids talked. In very few words, soft-spoken, they told our viewers what their experience had been like. They said it was hard to be forgotten. They didn't feel they'd been heard. They missed the teachers and classmates who'd died. One of the boys said what he had to say, paused, and then said it all over again in Dene. He wanted to make sure everyone back home who was watching could understand.

I was so struck by that. It was more than thoughtful; it was intentional. He knew who he was talking to and who mattered most: the people back home. Family and friends. I was bowled over by the quiet strength in these young people—their fearlessness. I don't know if I could have done what they had done. They'd walked into this facility full of journalists and reporters, and it was clear what they felt: *We're equal, and I am telling you my story. I challenge you not to respect me.*

I kept a sharp eye on them the whole time. I was in mama mode, protective, poised to jump in at any turn if someone looked uncomfortable, or pushed too hard, or treated them with anything less than courtesy and kindness. I was ready.

But there was no need for my fierce watchfulness. These kids were phenomenal. They handled that microphone like no adult I've ever seen.

Dene High comes to *The Social*, along with Raptors president Masai Ujiri (seated centre, next to me).

Stories of pain and triumph

The former beauty queen walked us down the Toronto street where she'd spent much of her time in the days when she was homeless and addicted to crack. A brief stint in jail and a judge who offered her a second chance changed the course of her life. She told us how she now counsels others caught in the same addiction spiral she'd managed to escape.

In an exclusive, leafy Toronto neighbourhood, over a cup of tea in a well-appointed living room, a lawyer described her ongoing battle with bipolar disorder, revealing how she'd bravely shared her struggles with her colleagues.

Over bowls of soup in the kitchen on the family farm, a young couple in Saskatchewan were candid about their difficulties. He suffered from anxiety. She faced postpartum depression. However, after speaking openly in their community about their problems, they'd faced online bullying: they had breached an unspoken rule that personal struggles weren't discussed publicly. Rather, as farmers, they ought to be tough, to just "suck it up, buttercup." Despite that backlash, slowly, over time, they'd noticed a shift. More people in the farming community had begun to come forward and relate their mental health issues. It was a start. A sign of hope.

These interviews were part of the program "In Their Own Words: A Bell Let's Talk Day Special," which I hosted and helped produce; it aired on CTV in prime time on January 31, 2018. Bell Let's Talk Day is a project of Bell Media, the parent company of CTV, which aims to widen the discussion on mental health, increase awareness around its prevalence and decrease the stigma attached to it. For many years, Bell Let's Talk had turned to celebrities such as TV personality Howie Mandel and Olympic gold medallist Clara Hughes, who publicly shared their stories about their mental health challenges, hopefully showing that no one is immune from such afflictions. No one is above them. This year, for the first time, the plan was to talk with ordinary Canadians from all walks of life about mental health. We wanted to hear from the farmer, the entrepreneur, the young student. We wanted to make it diverse in every single way: diversity of age, of race, of geographic location, of diseases suffered — so people could relate to them directly.

Four colleagues and I travelled from Halifax to Nunavut, visiting people in their homes. I was in the kitchens and living rooms and on the front porches of people across this country. I listened and learned as each of them talked with incredible honesty of their mental health struggles.

We met a successful business owner in Nova Scotia who suffered from obsessive-compulsive disorder. While we sat on stools in her kitchen, she told me how, in an effort to stop the voices in her head demanding perfection, she'd tried to kill herself. She showed me the tattoo on her wrist of two birds, one feeding the other. The image was symbolic of her two children. It was meant to hide the scars but also to remind her of how far she'd come.

A long journey from the east coast, way far north in Nunavut, was the openly transgender Métis teen who struggled with depression, anxiety and borderline personality disorder. Despite his struggles — and directly because of them — he's become a strong advocate for youth mental health awareness in his community. He shared his journey with us while sitting in his living room, and then we followed him to his high school to see what his average day was like.

Another young man took us to the intersection in Toronto where he was hit by a car at fifteen. He was fortunate to survive but suffered a traumatic brain injury. As he healed physically, he deteriorated mentally: sadness, anxiety and depression took over. He was diagnosed with post-traumatic stress disorder. He told us how he went on to study social work and now speaks publicly about PTSD at more than two dozen events every year.

I'm proud of the research I did, my part in producing that series. I'm proud of the solid interviews I conducted. It's about meeting people where they're at. Listening fully. But mostly I'm humbled. Sitting down with these people in their spaces as they shared their stories of pain and triumph was an honour.

I see this assignment as the best and most impactful one of my career. It's the piece of work I've heard the most about. People who watched it will still say to me, "Oh my goodness. I watched that special. I could relate to this, I went through that." As a team we produced a piece that made a difference and Canadians told us so. That's the feeling I want to have all the time. To know that what I'm a part of is helping someone somewhere.

Police stop

The couple of months during which we produced "In Their Own Words" was a tremendously busy time at work. In addition to working on the Bell Let's Talk Day Special and co-hosting a daily talk show, I'd also hosted the Santa Claus Parade with Melissa Grelo and, on top of that, worked on a network special with Jann Arden.

By the time February rolled around, I was exhausted and very much looking forward to a long weekend. I had driven Blaize to my sister's house for a sleepover with her cousins. My sister and Mom had gone out together to a banquet event. I was on my way back home to Lloyd and Dash. I remember being happy and looking forward to relaxing. As I pulled into my driveway, I saw the flashing lights.

The police officer got out of the car and headed toward mine.

I jumped out of my vehicle to see what the issue was. He told me forcefully to get back into my vehicle. His tone made me anxious. I quickly complied. As he approached the driver's side, he gestured for me to lower the window. I already had my licence and ownership waiting. I had grabbed them before he made his way to my truck. This is what Black people do. No false moves. Keep your hands where they can see them. Look the officer in the eye. As he was holding my ownership—where my address was clearly printed—he asked whether I lived here. I said yes. He said I had failed to stop at a stop sign. He said he'd be back.

I felt sick. This awful feeling in the pit of my stomach. I quickly called my sister. I wanted someone to know where I was and what was happening. I didn't call Lloyd, who was inside the house with Dash. I pictured him coming outside, being upset, and then who knows what might happen? He and Dash were safe in the house and I wanted it to stay that way.

When the officer returned, I told him that I'd been stopped in my neighbourhood a couple of times already over several months. That I'd been asked whether my vehicle was my vehicle. Whether I lived around here. Driving close to home, running errands on my off time, I was likely to be wearing Converse running shoes, a hoodie, maybe a pair of old jeans with rips in the knees. A ball cap. The officers who stopped me made me feel I didn't fit into this neighbourhood looking like that. What was I doing there? they seemed to imply. I told the officer on my driveway that I hadn't been given a ticket in any of these other stops. I said I was so tired of this. He just looked at me. I said to go ahead and give me a ticket. That if I'd done something wrong, I was more than happy to pay the price.

He said good night and walked away.

I took a few minutes to try to collect myself, and walked up to the house. As soon as I opened the front door, I fell apart. Dash, who was six years old at the time, asked why I was crying. I told him that an officer had stopped me on the driveway, and I was upset. Lloyd immediately went to the local precinct and came back with paperwork to file a report. While he was gone, I called my friend and co-host Lainey. Through tears, I asked her what I should do. Should I speak up? Go on social media?

"No," she said. "This deserves more. Write something, Marce. There isn't a newspaper in the country that wouldn't take a written piece about this from you."

I had never written a story for a paper, let alone a personal story. But as soon as Lainey brought it up, I knew it was the right thing to do. I contacted an editor at the *Globe and Mail*, who said he would take an op-ed piece.

I had scheduled a short getaway at a spa with my sister: work wasn't supposed to be a part of our retreat. But I spent the first day that we were there writing about the stop. It went back and forth between the editor and me. When it was finished, I alerted my senior managers at work, letting them know that it would be published the following Monday morning.

I knew that the piece would create a stir, but I wasn't prepared for the amount of vitriol that came my way. My story, "The Double Standard of Driving While Black—in Canada," trended across the country. There was support and lots of positive responses. There were kind people who wrote to thank me for the piece. Others wrote to share their own stories. Federal

Liberal MP Ahmed Hussen, then the minister of immigration, refugees and citizenship, told me of his experience being tailed by police on the way to a meeting in St. John's, Newfoundland. (He has made a TED Talk about this: the experience rattled him, bringing back his experience as a youth growing up in Toronto's Regent Park.) But those who claimed that I had broken the law and was now playing the "race card" were much louder.

"Go back to where you came from!"

"You should be fired!"

"You're a liar!"

Meanwhile, instead of reaching out to me, the Toronto Police Service used social media to get its message across. Toronto Police Staff Superintendent Mario Di Tommaso tweeted: "I have viewed the video footage of your vehicle stop. You were stopped because of your driving behaviour. You failed to stop at a stop sign. It was dark. Your race was not visible on the video and only became apparent when you stepped out of the vehicle on your drive way." Mike McCormack, then the president of Toronto Police Association, dug up an article in which I'd said that I "speed sometimes" to illustrate that my driving habits were suspect.

And the chief of police then Mark Saunders, called my workplace, wanting to speak to my superiors. My boss told him that the only person that he needed to speak to was me. My boss gave me Chief Saunders' phone number, and I called him. We decided to meet at a neutral location, an office at Ryerson University. An executive producer from CTV accompanied me. "I don't want you to go alone," she said. I was so grateful for her support.

When we arrived at the office, we met Chief Saunders, who was accompanied by another officer. The chief and I went into a private room. His first words were, "Marci, this is not racism."

I disagreed. I said that if I had rolled through a stop sign, then I was more than willing to pay a ticket. Why wasn't I stopped when the infraction happened? Why was I tailed to my driveway? Why was I asked whether I lived in my home while he was already holding my insurance and licence with my address clearly printed on both documents?

He was upset that I had talked about it on the show. He was upset that Lainey had reminded me on-air what I had said to her when I called her that night: that I'd feared for my life. I hadn't even remembered saying that until she brought it up. The fear was visceral.

What Chief Saunders, as well as those who'd had so much to say via social media, didn't bother to ask me was this simple question: "Why were you afraid?"

There is fear because a traffic stop isn't just a traffic stop. When it happens, thoughts of those who didn't survive them surge. As a reporter, I've seen more video and read more details than most people. There is a psychological toll to watching people who look like your dad, mom, sister, kids and nieces dying at the hands of police officers. Jermaine Carby, George Floyd, Ahmaud Arbery, Trayvon Martin, Andrew Loku, Tamir Rice, Sandra Bland, Michael Brown, Eric Garner, Regis Korchinski-Paquet . . . This is not just an American issue. A report by the Ontario Human Rights Commission published in the *Globe and Mail* in 2018 showed that Black people are twenty times more likely to be shot dead by police than white people. While Black people make up less than ten percent of Toronto's population, they were involved in seven out of ten fatal shootings by police. Robyn Maynard, author of *Policing Black Lives*, says this report reveals a disturbing truth: "When it comes to law enforcement, when it comes to the police, there is an overarching reality of violence that is often a part of the fabric of everyday life for Black people in this country. I think this data is absolutely damning and reveals something very important."

I know there are many good and fair police officers. But I also know that every Black man close to me has been stopped by police — and not for the right reasons. Maybe they were walking home late at night. Maybe the car they were driving was too flashy. Maybe, like my friend Dwight suggested, police were looking for someone whose description he matched. So there is a certain amount of anxiety that comes along with being stopped. Not to mention being stopped several times. It's interesting what happens when someone speaks out and that someone is a Black woman. The "angry" label is immediately applied to you. Who are you to speak up? Sit down. Know your place. Shut up. How dare you claim racism?

I never saw the tape. I didn't need to. I know how I felt. I know what was said. I don't regret coming forward, but I sometimes think that maybe I should have been a bit clearer in the piece I wrote for the *Globe*. The point was not whether I had rolled through a stop sign. I was perfectly willing to be issued a ticket if I'd committed a traffic violation. But that was where the story stopped for many people, who said I broke the law. Did they think I thought I was above it?

No, I didn't think I was above the law. The issue was not the ticket; it was what happened to me on my driveway. How I felt and how afraid I was. The devastation of being treated in what felt like an inhumane way—as if I didn't belong there. In my neighbourhood. Outside my own home. The ramifications of that moment—the fear I felt—continue to this day.

Conversations with my son

Dash, at eight, is a bundle of boldness, speed and light. I love all that about him. He tells people his name means "how you live your life."

I have never told my happy, full-of-life boy that I was scared to bring him into this world. I have a sister. She has three girls—my nieces—who I love like my own. I have a daughter, Blaize. But Dash is the first boy in our family. A Black boy. I cried when I learned he'd be a "he."

Being a Black female child seemed easier to me to navigate. Girls might get the benefit of the doubt. But a Black boy? I thought about the inevitable energy, curiosity, fearlessness. I imagined the conversations we'd have: *Always be respectful. Be kind, but stand your ground.* How when he became a teenager and wanted to borrow the car, I would smile while handing him the keys, hopefully hiding the fear I'd be feeling inside, and then watch my heart walking out the door. Where there would be no protection.

Even when Dash is uncertain, he moves forward.

I thought about the safety rules we'd have to lay down, hard. The careful conversation we'd have about when, not if, he was stopped by police. What to do. What not to do.

Place your hands where they are clearly visible.

Have your licence and registration ready so you don't have to reach for anything.

Look the officer in the eye when speaking.

I thought about the other conversations we'd have, about putting kindness and empathy first. But making it clear that kindness is not to be confused with weakness. So to be strong. Follow through on his convictions. Be proud of who he is and what he stands for—and more importantly, what he doesn't stand for.

We haven't gotten to some of these conversations yet. I'm still getting ready for them. Still grieving their necessity. No, I'm in a fury over their necessity.

I will tell Dash that the road will be harder for him than for many, that getting where he wants to get may take longer. But that his goals are valid. That he will attain them. And that if he fails, he must get right back up because the getting back up is what matters.

Above all else: stand.

Me with my son, Dash.

Stepping out

When I began working at *The Social*, an afternoon talk show, it was the first time in years that I wasn't literally getting up in the middle of the night to get to work on time.

I had a new lease on life.

It must have shown. At my friend Davinder's fiftieth birthday party, another old friend, Diane Lee Clemons, pulled me aside. "I've got this idea," she said. Her eyes showed excitement. "About doing a shoe line. Creating shoes."

"Wow," I said. "That's amazing."

There was a beat, and then she said, "What do you think about doing it with me?"

This wasn't like when I had to decide whether to move to Halifax for the job with CTV. Or whether to give up a huge chunk of my maternity leave to become a co-host on *Canada AM*. I knew right away the answer was a resounding yes. Absolutely, I wanted to do this.

And just like that, I became an entrepreneur.

Maybe it sounds weird that a business partnership would start this way. Just like that, boom. But it felt right. I had time. Creative energy. And I love shoes. I also love Di—who's kind, creative, really funky. We liked the idea of the two of us, women in our fifties or thereabouts—I wasn't quite fifty yet—launching a second career. The wife of Mike (Pinball) Clemons, the popular former football star, Di was a figure to contend with in her own right, a renowned singer and Juno nominee, philanthropist and motivational speaker. This project would be something new for her. And we loved the idea of developing the first Black female–owned footwear line in Canada.

So, we embarked on this thing. Marci Ien: Broadcaster. Journalist. Host. Shoe maven. Who knew? Who knows where life will take you? Diane had contacted George Sully, of the footwear and accessories company Sully Wong, who was a friend of one of her nephews. We brought him on to consult. He knew suppliers, had relationships with factories, and was able to advise us on the process of creating and bringing a product to market. We started small. We created what we called a capsule collection—one gorgeous, five-inch patent pump in three colours, with a leopard print on the soles, which would become our signature—for online order only. We called it the Sahara Collection.

In March 2017, we held a launch party. This happened to be the same week I'd written the op-ed piece for the *Globe and Mail* about being stopped by the police in my driveway. I remember getting dressed in the upper room of a restaurant and getting calls from the press—a reporter from the *Toronto Star,* another from the *Globe*—to ask for my comments about the backlash after the article ran. There were two hundred people downstairs waiting to celebrate with me. Upstairs, I spoke into the phone, attempting to master my emotions and put my thoughts into words that people would understand. It was like a surreal clash of realities.

Three years in, we've created, in a sense, a true family enterprise: small, co-operative and ambitious. Jennifer Branco, the executive director of the Pinball Clemons Foundation, has helped us with some marketing on the side. We've recruited our kids to help us with the social media angle. We've named new lines after our kids: the slip-on leisure bootie is called the Dash; our combat boot is the Blaize; the three slides in our Familia collection are named after Diane's daughters—Camille, Cymone and Chantel.

I can report having climbed a steep learning curve: We've made mistakes and learned from them. We know which way we lean in the perennial tussle of the fashion world; when choosing between the latest trends and our own personal taste, we go for what we like. Trends come and go, but you have to love what you're trying to sell. And we strive for a balance between affordability and quality—we don't want to price out the people we want to serve. It's a struggle. We've had a lot of heart-to-hearts: Is this really going to be successful? Do we have what it takes? We now understand that having a side hustle, as some people call an enterprise like ours, is like having another full-time job.

We also understand that to create a business, you have to have a good idea. There has to be dedication: you have to be all in. But you don't have to be an expert at everything yourself. You don't have to be all things. That's where help comes in. You lean on the people who've come before you. You have meetings. You ask questions. What did you do? What worked? What didn't? Tell me! You soak it all up like a sponge.

To a lifelong journalist and interviewer, it's familiar territory. This might be what's known as skill transference. When Diane and I launched IEN LEE, I had zero experience running a business. But I had an awful lot of practice gathering the info I needed to do what I had to do—and do it well.

My daughter, Blaize, and me, at the launch of IEN LEE.

The one with the orange door

Lloyd and I were definitely going to separate. It was real. We needed to sell the house. This was in May 2018. Blaize was starting high school in September. It made sense that, if we were going to make a big change, possibly move to a different part of the city, we should do it now.

By August, the house still hadn't sold. Lloyd had found a place for himself and put a down payment on it. He was moving out September 1. I needed a smaller place, and I needed it soon. I wanted the kids to be able to start the year in the same place where they'd finish it, not have to switch schools partway through.

I phoned my sister. Of course. Who else?

She said, "Don't worry. We're going to get this done."

She put her realtor chops to work, went online, checked

the listings, came up with a list of five or six suitable places for rent, and booked appointments. I met her the next morning. It was Sunday. The home we live in now was the third house we saw: a semi-detached house with an orange door in the heart of midtown Toronto.

I'd liked how it had looked in the listing: a little modern, lovely, welcoming. If you've ever gone house hunting, you know when you walk into a place if you can picture your family there. My sister and I walked through the house together. I looked in one of the bedrooms and thought, *This screams Dash*. I could picture my kids hanging out in the basement, playing Nintendo. There was a bathroom they could share, plus an ensuite in the master bedroom, which many semis don't have. We have a Shih Tzu terrier named Bella, and the yard was perfect for her.

If I rented this place, we'd be moving from suburbia, from a street with large houses spread out along it, to a bustling urban neighbourhood. I'd go from driving to get groceries and driving Blaize to dance class—driving everywhere, basically—to having coffee shops close by, places to go for dinner, a movie theatre. The freedom of that. I could immediately picture us there.

We could walk to a subway stop, which would be great for me to get to work. Even better, the house was within walking distance of both the kids' new schools. Because the neighbourhood was growing more dense, with condos being built and more families moving in, the local schools were limiting enrolment by address: odd house numbers were one catchment area, even house numbers another. The number on our house—Lorraine had made sure before even showing me the listing—matched the requirement for the school where I hoped to register Blaize, the one with a blended focus on arts and academics, which suited her interests and her strengths.

It just worked, all of it worked. Except—it stretched my budget. A little, not so much I couldn't manage. Still, it was a leap. I decided to take it. My sister got in touch with the agent. I had to provide a letter from my workplace, proving I was gainfully employed. Two days later, it was mine. We were able to move in well before September, so we had time to get settled for school. It had taken a mere few days to sort out. That's the power of Lorraine in action.

The other house, though, didn't sell for a couple more months. Lloyd and I split the expenses of maintaining it. It was a hard fall. The realities of a life transition aren't just emotional: they're practical. They're financial. But we made it through. You just do. And then you look back and think, *Wow. That was rough. But we did it. And look at us now.*

Thirteen (part two)

I'd tried so hard to be what my parents weren't. We all try to be different from our parents in some way, don't we? I was determined my marriage would be better than theirs had been. We would talk. We would support each other. We would be a team.

We would stay together.

But, it turns out, we didn't stay together. We hadn't been a team—at least not the kind I'd needed. We'd put the house up for sale, and I'd moved to the place with the orange door that my sister had helped me find. The kids were going back and forth between the two houses. At first, until we were ready to broach this with them, we explained that we needed to take care of both places until the old place sold. But after a month of this, the kids were starting to ask why Dad never came to stay at the new house and why none of the furniture from there was coming here. They were confused and wondering. It was time.

On a Saturday morning, I drove out to the suburbs to pick up some more things to bring back to my place. We all sat down together as a family in the living room of the house we'd lived in for twelve years. Blaize was thirteen, the same age I'd been when my dad had told me he and my mom were splitting up. Dash was six. This was the only house he knew.

I started talking. I said, "You know how much we love you, but Dad and I aren't going to be together. We're going to separate because things aren't working out between us. But you will always come first. We love you. You'll have two houses to go to." And so on. Blaize said nothing. She stood and walked out of the room and went for a walk, tears in her eyes. Dash just sat there—my son, who never stops moving. My kids were in pain, and I had put them there.

Blaize needed some time. When she came back, I wrapped my arms around her. I said, "I got you forever." Lloyd was quiet. He'd told me earlier that I was breaking up our family. That this wasn't what he wanted. But this wasn't about him or the kids. This was about me. I was trying to save myself.

Later, Blaize said to me that she had sensed something was wrong—just as I had, on reflection, about my parents when they split up. Sometimes she heard us argue. She knew something wasn't right. She said, "It's better to have two happy homes than one unhappy one."

That was a wise thing to say. Our kids are sometimes wiser than we are.

We the North

In 2019, when the Toronto Raptors beat Milwaukee and stamped their ticket to the finals, Blaize and I were watching. The win was exhilarating. We jumped in my car and hit Yonge Street to join the celebration. People were spilling out of bars, running through the streets, honking up a storm, and shouting "Let's go, Raptors!" Way downtown, in Jurassic Park, the nickname for the public square outside Scotiabank Arena where the Raptors play, thousands of Torontonians had already gathered: all through the playoffs, games were broadcast on a giant outdoor screen. Streams of people filled the square and the nearby streets.

Making the finals was one thing. When the Raptors actually beat the Golden State Warriors *in* Golden State, when their historic 2019 NBA championship win was sealed by Kawhi

Leonard's free throws, we hit Yonge again. It was nuts. People were honking, high-fiving. Someone had climbed up a street light. One guy tried to jump on our car.

Back at work, there was talk of a victory parade. The planning would be fast, as it would take place within the week. When my boss called me in and said, "We want you on the coverage team," I was thrilled. The organizers at CTV wanted it to be personal, for the emotion of the day to really resonate with viewers. Tyrone Edwards of the entertainment newsmagazine *etalk* would be on the mainstage at the rally at the parade's end, interviewing Drake. I would follow the parade from its starting point at Exhibition Place and interview Masai Ujiri along the way.

The lead-up to the championship, and the widespread enthusiasm (long overdue, in my opinion!) building around the team, had been exciting—and, for me, busy. It wasn't just keeping up with the games. It wasn't just the emotion of seeing so many people jump on board and the team finally win so many hearts. I was doing radio interviews; people knew I'd been saying for years that the Raptors are Canada's team—the only NBA team in the country—and they knew the story of my dad and me going to games together every week. I was clearly the fan for the job.

The morning of the parade, a hot June day, I reported to a huge parking lot near the Princes' Gates at the Exhibition Place grounds. Floats and dignitaries were mustering for the victory march that would wend along Lake Shore Boulevard West, then north along Toronto's grand University Avenue, and finally several blocks along Queen Street West to City Hall, where a rally would take place midday in Nathan Phillips Square.

As the parade got underway, I walked alongside the car that Masai rode in with his wife, Ramatu, and their children, my camera operator following along and catching our interview-on-the-move. I said to him, "You said you were going to build a championship team and people laughed. They said, 'OK, buddy, dream on.'"

We had time, moving at parade speed, for a lengthy interview. We talked about how Masai had built the team in an unconventional way, taking risks. Often teams succeed by drafting amazing players, the way Cleveland drafted LeBron James back in the day, or the Lakers drafted Kobe Bryant. But the Raptors didn't become champions through the draft process. They didn't have the money. And they had Masai, who thought outside the box and looked for talent outside the normal places. Instead of looking for star talent chiefly at American universities, he brought in players from Spain, from the Congo, from Senegal. He brought the Raptors 905, an NBA development league team, into being in Mississauga in 2015, defying conventional wisdom that our tax system, as well as possible visa issues for American players, would make a Canadian-based franchise untenable. A couple of our best players came up through that team. The whole culture of the Toronto Raptors is one of building something out of nothing, making do, finding new ways to seek out talent. Outside of Kawhi Leonard, this championship team wasn't made up of superstars—and he didn't win this championship on his own. Masai had taken chances. He'd fired a coach who won Coach of the Year. He'd traded Toronto's most beloved player. If this didn't work, if it blew up, he could have lost his job. It was such an honour to talk to him that day, to take in the city as we marked his team's success.

Until a certain point, the day is a blur of joy, that rare occasion when your worlds come together: your favourite thing to do in your downtime and your profession. How do you even call that work? I rode along on one of the team's double-decker buses through streets lined with cheering crowds that were so large people were pressing in close around the bus. More than two million people lined the streets of Toronto that day. I saw people's noses pressed against their office windows along the route. Construction workers sat on their machines waving "We the North" flags.

I interviewed Jamaal Magloire while riding along on his float with his family. He's from Scarborough, like I am, went to Eastern Commerce High School and became a star player at the University of Kentucky before playing in the NBA for several years. Now a coach with the Raptors, he's special to both the Scarborough community and the Black community. I was able to talk with him about what it means to be a Canadian and about the position he's in now—how far he's come from his start as a Scarborough kid.

I spoke with parents in the crowd, saying to them cheekily, "So, you pulled your kids out of school." They replied, "Absolutely! This is history." Some of them said there are different ways to learn, and this is one. These were people whose kids hadn't been born yet when the Raptors got their start—but the parents sure had been.

The happiness was palpable that day. It was just euphoric. People were giddy with pride.

And then, as we all know, the celebration was marred by a shooting at Nathan Phillips Square. Three suspects were arrested in a dramatic takedown. Four people were wounded. Others fled for cover. Trying to get home afterward was unbelievable. I walked toward the Eaton Centre. The Bay was closed because the police were looking for a fourth suspect. The Queen Street subway station was closed. I had to continue walking—up Yonge Street amid this huge, anxious crowd, partners with kids, a sea of humanity, all of us wanting to be home. I went past Dundas and College stations, Wellesley, then Bloor.

Aside from my shock and my unease as I slowly made my way up Yonge Street, block after long, hot, crowded block, the Black woman side of me was just crushed. I thought, *Can't we have nice things?* Part of the thrill of the Raptors winning so many hearts was the diversity of the team and the fans. They're mostly Black players on the court. And the crowd in the stands is way more diverse than at a Leafs game. That's what was so beautiful about the crowds gathering at Jurassic Park: it looked like the United Nations. And they could see themselves in those players.

For any people who look at basketball and think it's just a bunch of mostly Black guys running up and down a court, I look at the NBA and I think, *This is a league that leads.* From an entrepreneurial standpoint, the people who run this league are brilliant. The way they have expanded this game internationally is so far beyond what hockey, football or baseball has even attempted. Even with something like the coronavirus pandemic, they didn't joke around. One player's infected: shut it down. They were the first professional sports league to respond so decisively and proactively. The NBA led, and everybody followed. This leadership doesn't joke around. You've got to like that.

And so the Raptors, the once-scoffed-at Toronto basketball team, win the NBA championship and the city comes out to party. It's incredible, beyond anything you might have imagined. And then this thing happens. There's a shooting. And I'm thinking, *Oh good God. Everybody who thinks disparaging things about people of colour—that's all been validated right now.* There's that side of it. The side of me that wants to say, *Can't we just prove people wrong? Can we just not do that in this grand, global space we've created to showcase this wonderful thing we've made?*

That day went from the highest of highs to the lowest of lows. It brought the best and the worst of human nature to light. When I think back on that day, Toronto in all its diversity seemed to erupt with joy; the entire parade felt like hope and possibility come to life. I want to rub away that violent blot at the end of the long, happy, cheer-fuelled route we travelled. But I can't.

All I can do is remind myself how far the Raptors' fiercely proud basketball fans have come, how many Torontonians and Canadians we've brought onside, and what new triumphs may be in store.

A friendship is sparked

A sorrow that had nothing to do with basketball, violence or racism floated lightly around me as I moved through the streets the day of the Raptors parade. For the seeds of that sorrow, we need to go back a few years, to the days of *Canada AM* and the morning I interviewed graphic novelist Teva Harrison.

Let me start by saying that I love my job. I love asking people questions—not just politicians or celebrities or people in power. I love asking people questions, period: anyone who has something to say. I want to learn about who they are, why they made certain decisions, what's important to them, what they regret. Their hopes, their fears, their hard-won secrets for survival or success.

But a great interview doesn't ride on enthusiasm alone. It's a real art to do an interview well, to pose a series of questions in a way that creates, for the viewer or listener, an exchange that sounds and feels like a naturally flowing conversation. One that goes unexpected places and contains moments of insight or revelation. One that makes it impossible not to keep listening and not to take something meaningful away. This kind of interview takes skill, especially with a subject who's practised at sticking to their "script," or with someone who's slightly nervous or less than forthcoming. Even with the best training and years of practice, an interview doesn't always work as well as you'd hope.

On the other hand, there are times when a real connection takes place during an interview—when I can feel a fizz of energy in that space between my questions going out and the answers coming back.

Occasionally, a friendship is sparked.

When Teva Harrison walked into the *Canada AM* studio, her smile made me smile. She held out her hand and I grasped it. Her presence warmed up the room—not a small feat in a big, brightly lit studio riddled with camera equipment, tripods and cables. I thought, *This woman isn't sick. What do you mean?*

I told her we'd have seven minutes to chat.

Teva, at thirty-seven, had been diagnosed with metastatic breast cancer. She'd documented her journey with terminal illness in the graphic memoir *In-Between Days*, which was shortlisted for a Governor General's Literary Award in 2016. She was living with death knocking at her door. She'd recently been married. She and her husband had purchased their first home. She had people and things to live for. She wanted desperately to live. But the prognosis was not in her favour.

She was open about her situation, much like the pictures she'd drawn for her book. I was struck by her approach to her diagnosis. She knew she only had a limited number of days. She called these her "in-between days" and said she intended to make the most of them. Her philosophy reminded me of my dad's message about the dash. I so liked her. She was matter of fact, direct. She was brave. I didn't want our seven minutes to end. I could have talked to her all day. I think, in truth, they gave me some extra time. I took as much as they'd allow.

We kept in touch through the years that followed, mostly over social media. I remember her being in New York, winning an award for her book. I saw on Twitter that she was at a beach somewhere, soaking up the sun. I'd send her little notes: *Thinking of you* or *Glad you're doing well*. We kept making plans to get together, but something—usually her illness—would get in the way. In December 2018, I gave it another shot:

Me: Teva. Thinking of you always. Are you in town for the holidays? Can we meet?

Teva: Dear Marci, I will be home next week and would love to see you.

Me: How is next Saturday the 22nd?

Teva: That would be perfect. I'm free the early half of the day. Would that work for you?

Me: That's perfect. Looking forward.

Me: Teva, is it easier if I just came to you? To your place?

Teva: I hesitate because it is SUPER messy in my house. Between chemo and travel, I just haven't been cleaning. How much of that can you tolerate? Haha. Maybe we should just go out. I really don't mind coming to you, though, if there's a place you love.

Teva: Hi from the middle of the night. I've been up all night sick because of the chemo and I'm going to have to reschedule. I'm really sorry for the late notice and I hope we can easily find another time. I'm so sorry.

Me: My darling Teva. I am sending you so much love. Of course we will find another time. Stay in touch. I've been thinking of you so much.

Teva: Thank you so much for understanding. I'm on my last round of chemo before I get a break, so please let's rebook soon.

Me: You let me know when. I can't wait to see you.

Me: Hi love. How are you? Thinking of you.

Teva: Hi again! I have a new puppy. Can we make plans at my house instead of a café? I hate leaving him alone. He's just a baby.

That was the last text I got from Teva. February 20, 2019. We never did manage to make those plans. She died two months later. I didn't know at first. I was at work—with *The Social* by then—and ran into my friend Katie Jamieson, the producer of the *Canada* AM segment on which Teva and I had met, in the washroom. She told me that Teva had passed away. I froze. We had failed to get together. I'd let too much time pass.

Teva Harrison died on April 28, 2019, at the age of forty-two. Her memorial service was set for June 17, the same day I was assigned to follow the Raptors' victory parade through the streets of downtown Toronto. My plan was to attend the service, which was later in the afternoon. So even amid my rapture that day, there was this anticipation of the farewell I'd be making later on as I'd join with so many others in honouring the marvel that was Teva, this woman who had written that she wanted to "live like a tornado."

But when the parade fell so far behind schedule, I finally had to face reality. I just wasn't going to make it. I was crushed. I never got to say goodbye. I hold Teva's memory, and my memory of that smile coming at me as she walked toward me through the studio, close. I'm constantly reminded, having been touched by her rich, unforgettable "in-between" days, to make the most of mine.

Black woman off script

I was done. No more, I said. I'm off Twitter. I've had enough. I can't do this anymore.

Blaize—that amazing young woman who happens to be my daughter—spoke up right away. "But Mom," she said, "we *need* your voice there."

This kid of mine. Her wisdom. Her power. Her insistence on holding her ground. Her jaw-dropping courage.

Like many teens, Blaize has struggled with mental health. Each summer, she and Dash go to an overnight camp for a few weeks. One year, the summer after Lloyd and I separated, I received a call from the camp doctor informing me Blaize was feeling low, having trouble fitting in. When we arrived soon after that call for a weekend visit—Lloyd and I together, as we'd always done—we had to cajole her to come out for a family lunch with us, a tradition the four of us had always loved. We did go out, and we talked, and her distress was so deep—some of it related to how we'd handled our separation, a truth that was hard for me to hear—that three months later, we were sitting together in the office of a psychiatrist specializing in youth mental health. Blaize is much improved these days, far more herself, but she still sees a therapist. And I still worry, and do my best to listen, to give her the space she needs so she can be open and honest about how she's doing. I try to learn where she's coming from, what life looks like from her perspective—to not impose my own expectations and fears, as her mother, onto her.

Youth is fraught with challenges no matter what. But we all know the minefield of adolescence is riddled with far more danger zones now that we have Twitter, Instagram, Snapchat and so on—now that the ways to be shunned, bullied and scorned have ballooned. Now that kids can't as easily come home and tune out, turn off, enter a private space of refuge away from the relentless pressures of the social scene. With social media, the rules have somehow changed. The reach of the judgment of your peers has changed.

And yet, when Blaize has been dealing with something tough—say, the period in her life when she was coming home from school for lunch because she had no one to sit with—she's given me her unconditional permission to talk about it openly on-air with my co-hosts on *The Social*. Not just her permission but her encouragement. She *wants* me to talk about these things. She'll say, "I can't be the only one. There are other people having this experience, and it might make them feel better to know they aren't alone."

I find her remarkably brave. And stalwart. Where, some-times, I falter. When I was a co-host on *Canada AM*, when I was reading the news headlines from a teleprompter, my social media threads—save the odd crank—were relatively calm, supportive, tame environments. Now that I'm on a talk show where I share my opinions, and where I sometimes raise unpleasant issues such as racism or other forms of social injus-tice, the ire and vitriol that comes my way is breathtaking. What's worse is that some of it is directed at Blaize, who wades in, fearlessly calling out—with measured comments such as "Quick and friendly reminder that reverse racism does not exist!"—those who think hiding behind a digital platform gives them permission to ignore any form of social decency, reason-ableness or kindness.

As a small sampler, I've been told on Twitter that I've ruined my kid. That it's no wonder my husband dumped me. That I promote racist ideology, that I use social media to "promote my segregated world view" and my "belief" that "everyone is racist" against me. There was this: "Please read the signs and don't feed the animals." And this: "I'll let her explain why Lloyd tossed her to the curb." And this: "Mom's little racist is growing up fast." Here's a doozy from early May 2020: "When @MarciIen looks back at her life she will realize that it was only when she was on @TheSocialCTV that negativity sur-rounded her." Those tagged include fellow CTV journalists and hosts, from my former *Canada AM* colleagues Bev Thom-son and Jeff Hutcheson—who felt compelled to tweet back in my defence—as well as CTV executives.

This last one is telling, and to explain why is to raise an

issue that the hate-mongers on Twitter don't like to hear. Barack Obama put it best in a widely quoted comment from the Michael Jordan documentary *The Last Dance*. Obama said, "Any African American that sees significant success has an added burden. America is very quick to embrace a Jordan, an Oprah, or a Barack Obama, so long as it's understood you don't get too controversial around broader issues of social justice."

The problem is this: I'm a Black woman off script, speaking my mind. And my mind sometimes wants to speak frankly about the experience of being Black, or other-than-white, in this country, which isn't the racism-free zone that's part of our national mythology. So when I tell listeners I was afraid when a police officer pulled me over in my own driveway, when I offer my opinions on issues such as the lack of safe water and the high suicide rates in so many Indigenous communities, when I question the fairness of a policy or spending plan, I am perceived as overstepping. As having broken some unspoken agreement with a certain segment of the viewing population. Those who would tweet, "We used to like you on *Canada* AM" or "She is a caricature of who she once was. #cancelthesocial."

What is the good in engaging in a realm that allows, and even rewards, such verbal abuse? The good is just as Blaize has put it to me: to be the other voice. The voice we need to hear in the face of bigotry, judgment and hate—a voice people need to be reminded exists. There are so many ways to insult a person online, to reduce them to a facsimile of a human being, an "other" to be pelted with cruelty. But the thing is, so much good happens online as well: people are supportive, caring. They pipe up with likes and loves. They become each other's spontaneous cheerleaders. They offer pep talks and pick-me-ups. And they play. They share songs, dances, photos, laughs.

It's easy to forget the far more plentiful camaraderie and kindness, which is really what draws us online. I think of a particular tweet that was posted after my marriage ended, and I'd spoken about it on the air. Now that I'm on this show where I'm not just permitted but *encouraged* to speak openly, I strive to be frank about the difficulties I face in life. I agree with Blaize: it might help someone else to hear about my struggles. One viewer did not see it that way, however. The tweet read, "@TheSocialCTV omg! @MarciIen was always my fav perfect Canadian professional woman hero! Working, wife, mom, kids, family, etc., face of perfection goals! Now you are separated?? Heartbreak! Shattered!"

As in, I failed this person. Let them down. Am not the person they thought I was.

I won't lie. That tweet hurt. But I remind myself that that kind of hurt, flung through cyberspace, is like a slap. It shocks. It stings. I can allow it to leave a mark, or I can shake it off, swat it away.

Ultimately, I don't care about "failing" the person behind this tweet. I care about failing my daughter and others like her. And so, I won't walk away from this sometimes maddening, deeply troubled—and troubling—digital space. Not yet.

A friend in quarantine

For nearly two weeks, I've been sending little texts to my friend Karina.

"I'm here whenever you want to talk."

"I'm thinking of you, sending love."

"I'm praying right now. I'm here."

Sometimes she'll answer, sometimes she won't. I send the messages so she knows that, from what seems like an impossible distance, in an impossible situation, I'm with her. She isn't alone.

I was her fan before soccer legend Karina LeBlanc became my friend. She played for Canada in five FIFA Women's World Cups, two Pan American Games and two Olympic Games, bringing home the Olympic bronze medal in 2012. I watched Karina play for our country over the years. I thought she was amazing. A leader and an incredible athlete.

In 2015, before the FIFA World Cup, Karina announced she was retiring from international soccer, having been one of the longest-serving players in Canadian soccer history. The first interview she gave after that announcement was on *Canada* AM. Transitions, those moments in life that reveal so much about who we are and who we can be. Bev conducted the interview, and I watched and listened, as riveted as any viewer.

Karina told a story about her team coach once sitting the players down and asking them who they thought they were. "Who are you, Karina LeBlanc?"

"I'm a soccer player."

He shook his head. No, he said. You're not a soccer player. You have other gifts. You're gifted to lead, the way you've led this team. Your gift is to inspire, the way you've inspired young girls across this country and beyond.

Karina was trying to figure out what to do now, how to find her place in the world post soccer, how to find her voice. And the coach's message, coming back to her, gave her a new perspective, something to think about. Instead of feeling stymied, she was looking forward to determining her next steps.

She spoke of that exchange with the coach in later interviews, too. In 2017, she said to a reporter about the coach, "He basically said to me, 'If you think your purpose on this Earth is to kick a soccer ball for Canada, then I've failed you. You have something that is more than just the sport.' And it triggered me.

And it made me ask myself, 'Why am I here? What is my purpose in this world?'"

Before her *Canada AM* interview, Karina had asked me if she could talk to me after the show. I said of course. So she stuck around until we'd wrapped up for the day and came back into the dark studio after everybody else had left. We sat down in some comfy chairs and talked for an hour and a half. She was looking for my thoughts and advice as she considered possible career pathways: maybe public speaking, maybe hosting events, maybe some television. We talked about her life so far, how she was born in Atlanta, Georgia, lived in the Caribbean, but mostly grew up in BC, and what that was like. We talked about the team. We talked about a pivotal event in her youth—when she was cut from a soccer team. Her dad had said to her at the time, "You have to work for what you want." She took that to heart and was never cut from a team again.

The more I listened, the more we talked, the more I admired and liked her. We became fast friends. She told me later how important that talk was to her, two Black women alone in deep conversation about career and life and how to make the most of what you have to offer. She said, "You were what I wanted to be, and you were willing to help me." She said it meant so much there was no sense of competition, that I sent the clear message there was room for all of us to find success. Something I barely remember saying made such an impact on her that she sometimes quotes it when she gives speeches. I had said, "What's meant for me is meant for me. What's meant for you is meant for you."

• • •

Less than a year later, I was invited to a tennis tournament in Charleston, South Carolina, the largest women's-only tennis tournament in North America. Lisette, a Montreal clothing company whose pants became major fashion items after Oprah donned them on the cover of one of her magazines, was one of the event's sponsors. I had become friends with the husband-and-wife entrepreneurial team who own the company, Lisette Limoges and Neil Small, after they'd appeared on *Canada AM* and their marketing director, Debbie Benchimol, and I had hit it off. I was encouraged to bring a guest to the tournament. I called Karina. We didn't know each other that well yet. It felt a little crazy to ask, but I did. It seemed like a good chance for a girls' weekend. And it involved sports. She immediately said, "Yeah, I'll go." So we took the trip together, shared a room and bonded. It was so much fun. We talked about our goals, our dreams, where we wanted to be in the next year and beyond. By the time we flew home a few days later, she felt like a sister.

Fast-forward four years, to early 2020, smack in the midst of the COVID-19 pandemic. Karina and her husband are in the Bahamas, where they now have a house. She moved to Miami from Canada's west coast in 2018 when she accepted the position of head of women's soccer for CONCACAF, the Confederation of North, Central American and Caribbean Association Football, one of FIFA's six continental governing bodies. She had to think hard about it because she had, actually, begun to build a career around the very possibilities we'd talked over in the studio that day: public speaking and broadcasting. She'd done sports commentary during the Olympic Games and still regularly appears on CBC. She'd done motivational speaking, had addressed United Nations General Assembly panels and hosted major events such as TEDx in Vancouver in 2018. Taking the job with CONCACAF would mean putting the brakes on the new path she'd forged for herself as well as shifting gears and direction. But she felt she could make a difference in women's soccer, so she took the job.

A year or so later, Karina became pregnant. She gave birth to a healthy girl in late March 2020, just as the coronavirus was sweeping across the world, causing cities, regions and entire nations to virtually lock down and keep everyone but essential workers at home. At the time, to adhere to the directives of physical distancing here in Canada, my co-hosts and I were all collectively taping *The Social* each day in our own living rooms, a technologically fussy endeavour and a surreal, oddly quiet experience compared to our usual daily programs aired live with a studio audience.

Like so many others working from home, I felt lucky to have my job at all, as workers across the country faced layoffs and entrepreneurs feared for the future of their businesses. I felt lucky to be able to self-isolate while health care professionals and other essential workers were out there working every day. But also like so many others working from home, my kids were off school, routines were out the window, anxiety was high, and ordinary days had become these strange new worlds to navigate. I worried for my parents, longed to see my sister, and was in anguish over the effects the virus was having on the most vulnerable members of our society.

I also thought daily about Karina, way down south in the Bahamas.

The birth had gone fine, but at home not long after, Karina found herself not feeling well. She woke up in the middle of the night wheezing, short of breath. The next morning, her doctor told her over the phone to get to the hospital straightaway. When she went, she was immediately admitted with a condition that, if not promptly treated, might have proved fatal. She stayed overnight but in the morning received a call from her doctor, who said that things had changed quickly: even she wasn't permitted to come to the hospital. She wanted Karina out of there.

It turned out a patient with coronavirus had checked in the night before and then died. So Karina was discharged, but her instructions were to immediately go home and isolate herself—not just from the outside world but from her newborn. That meant also from her husband, who would have to care for the baby alone during that time.

For fourteen days, Karina stayed in a room in their house alone. Her husband brought her meals and set up a baby monitor so she could see their daughter.

Karina didn't want to talk while she was in quarantine: It was too much. She was too emotional. It's hard when you can't be there for a friend—in person, or even on the phone. But this wasn't the time to be there for her in that way. It was my job to let her know I had her back; that I would listen if she needed an ear; soothe and comfort if she wanted either; even provide distracting chatter if that was the ticket—but not to turn my support into any kind of burden. The trick was to offer presence and caring without riders: no pressure to share or reassure. No expectation of divulgences or heart-to-hearts. I knew Karina would reach out when she needed to, wanted to, was ready to. I just kept sending those texts.

Thank God for texts.

"I'm here with you. Sending love. Everything will be OK."

The day before Karina's isolation was to end, when at long last she'd be allowed to hold her baby again, she sent me a message.

"Can you talk later?"

Absolutely, I told her. Name the time. I'm here.

Me and Karina LeBlanc on her wedding day.

Bearing witness

Sometimes you need to stand in a place to understand what happened there. Is this the natural instinct of the journalist? Perhaps.

When Karina and I travelled to Charleston, we watched fabulous tennis, ate great meals and explored the historic city (which wasn't exactly uplifting: it was once a major centre of the slave trade in North America). We also wanted to visit Emanuel African Methodist Episcopal Church, where, just months before, nine African Americans were killed by a white supremacist in a mass shooting during a Bible study. The twenty-one-year-old shooter had been invited to join the study group before he turned his weapon on his hosts.

Karina and I wanted to see the place where this atrocity had occurred. To be there in body and to think about the meaning of this hate crime. To pay our respects to the lives lost. We hailed a cab and asked the driver to take us there. It was a neat, white building with peaked roofs, archways and a tall spire. The door was unlocked. Inside you could still feel the heaviness. A custodian greeted us warmly. I asked him if people were still coming to services. He said they were, but the numbers weren't back to what they'd had before. He invited us to come to the Sunday service. Karina and I looked at each other and instantly agreed.

So we found ourselves sitting in a pew on Sunday morning, our presence embraced. The people were so generous and kind. And as I sat there, feeling the amazing spirit of that congregation, I could picture the whole scenario. Of course they'd welcomed that young man into the church. We'd walked in on a Friday afternoon and here we were, invited back, being treated as if we belonged. Like part of the family.

For the congregation to remain so open and accepting so soon after that tragic and violent betrayal of their kindness spoke volumes to me. Of goodness. Of bravery. Of what it truly means to stand your ground.

Alone

Aloneness is a sense of comfort and ease when you're in your own company. On the other hand, when you're lonely, you become your own worst enemy.

—Sam Woolfe

One of my best friends always corrects me when I say that I'm lonely.

You aren't lonely, Marci. You're alone. There's a difference. You have people who love you. Who want the best for you. Family and friends. You need to remember that.

You might feel lonely, but alone is not a bad place to be. Being alone is about getting back in touch with your own self. Getting comfortable in your own skin. Another word for this is solitude.

I had been a wife for almost twenty years. It was a big part of who I was. Stepping out of that mould and making my own way is hard. I have to face things that I've buried. Own up to the fact that I was part of a dysfunctional equation.

Stand. Heal. Move forward.

It's not always easy. My closest friends have partners. Their relationships seem solid. I sometimes want what they have. I wonder if I ever will.

But my friend is right. I have my family, and I have my friends. And I have myself. Who sometimes feels lonely. Who craves the companionship of a giving partner. Who wonders and wishes. But who's busy getting to know herself again. Discovering things she maybe never knew. Looking forward, looking back. Being here, right here, happy with who she is, yet pushing onward. Asking. Listening. Relishing. Learning.

Acknowledgements

I had been thinking about writing a book for years but often wondered whether I had enough of a story to tell. It turns out, it wasn't about one story. My life so far has been about many of them. It is also one thing to think about writing a book and quite another to actually do it. That takes focus, honesty and the support of family and friends. Thanks to my sister, Lorraine, who is my rock. To my nieces, Melayna, Jordanne and Sari: I am grateful to be your aunt. You are extraordinary. To Blaize and Dash: Thank you for teaching me every day. You are my biggest blessings. To my parents: Thank you for showing me how to work hard but, above all, respect others. To Uncle Maurice: Thanks for being my second dad. To Barb: Thank you for your loving and caring spirit. To Lainey, Cynthia, Jess and Mel: Thank you for your warmth, friendship and legendary sleepovers. I love you. To Erin: Thank you for your friendship and wisdom. To Deb: Life changed when I met you. Here's to more adventures. To Petrina, the kindest person I know. Thanks for loving me well. To Donovan: Thank you for your endless support. To David Leonard: Thank you for sending me Teva's beautiful words to use as the epigraph for the book. Finally, to Brad and Anita: You are brilliant and asked me all the right questions. There is no book without you.